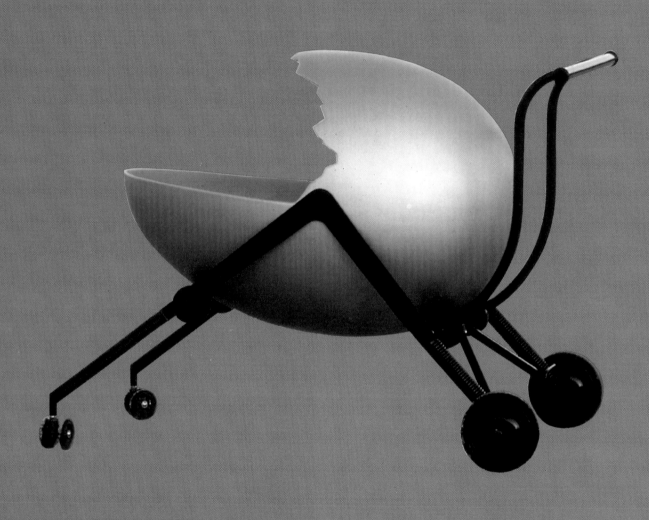

JAPAN DESIGN

Matthias Dietz · Michael Mönninger

TASCHEN

UMSCHLAGVORDERSEITE / FRONT COVER / COUVERTURE
Getsuen, 1990
Sessel, chair, chaise

Design Masanori Umeda

UMSCHLAGRÜCKSEITE / BACK COVER / COUVERTURE
Primitive Android
Fernsehgerät, television set, appareil de télévision

Design Shozo Toyohisa

FRONTISPIZ / FRONTISPIECE / FRONTISPICE
Yuné, 1988
Kinderwagen, baby carriage, landau

Design Yutaka Hikosawa

© 1992 Benedikt Taschen Verlag GmbH
Hohenzollernring 53, D-5000 Köln 1
Edited by Matthias Dietz,
Dietz Design Management, Frankfurt
Text: Michael Mönninger, Frankfurt
Design: Rafael Jiménez & Claudia Casagrande, Frankfurt
English translation: Michael Hulse, Cologne (main text);
Doris Linda Jones, Frankfurt (captions)
French translation: Michèle Schreyer, Cologne
Reproductions: Krefting & Melcher, Düsseldorf

Printed in Italy
ISBN 3-8228-9350-1

INHALT

CONTENTS

SOMMAIRE

VORWORT
Fumio Shimizu

PREFACE
Fumio Shimizu

PREFACE
Fumio Shimizu

Dieses Buch stellt zeitgenössisches »japanisches Design« vor. Zwar entstammen die meisten dieser Gestalter der sehr aktiven »Commercial und Interior Design«-Szene, aber auch avantgardistische Designer wie Shiro Kuramata oder Shigeru Uchida werden vorgestellt. Insgesamt hat das japanische Design durch seine sehr individualistischen Expressionen erfrischend neue Werke hervorgebracht, die die Design-Szene weit über Japan hinaus bereichert haben.

Das Design im Japan der sechziger Jahre wurde, wie in anderen Ländern auch, stark von der Pop Art geprägt. Die Zeichnungen der englischen Architektengruppe »Archigram« ebenso wie das italienische »Radical Design« von Gruppen wie »Archizoom«, »Superstudio« oder »Global Tools« beeinflußten auch das zeitgenössische japanische Design.

Wer das gestalterische Erbe der sechziger Jahre in Japan wirklich verwaltete, waren die »Interior Designer«. Die erste Hälfte der siebziger Jahre war die Zeit, in der sich die japanische Modewelt eine eigenständige Position aufbaute. Spezifisch japanische Marken wie Comme des Garçons und Issey Miyake entstanden und verlangten für ihre angemessene Präsentation besondere Räume.

Die so vor konkrete Aufgaben gestellten Interior-Designer brachten revolutionäre Ergebnisse hervor. Besonders seit den siebziger Jahren, obwohl noch vom traditionellen japanischen Interior Design inspiriert, interpretierten sie den »Primary Structure«- und »Minimal Art«-Stil neu und schufen so eine spezifisch japanische Ausdrucksform. Dies zeigt sich vor allem in der frühen Arbeit von Shigeru Uchida in den siebziger Jahren. Seine Werke neutralisieren die Form als solche und beseitigen das Gefühl der Existenz konkreter Gegenstände, seine Werke verweigern sich aber gleichzeitig nicht dem Alltagsleben, der Realität, sondern in ihnen entfaltet sich ein spezifischer, pulsierender Minimalismus.

Seit den achtziger Jahren entwickelt sich Japan zu einer affluenten Konsumgesell-

This book provides an overview of contemporary Japanese design. Although most of the designers presented here come from the very active commercial and interior design scene, the creations of avant-garde designers such as Shiro Kuramata or Shigeru Uchida are also included. On the whole, the highly individualistic expressions of Japanese design have brought a refreshing element to the scene and enriched the world of design far beyond the island realm of Japan.

During the 1960s, design in Japan, as in other countries, was strongly influenced by Pop Art. The drawings of the English group of architects, »Archigram« as well as Italian »radical design« by such groups as "Archizoom", have also had an impact on contemporary Japanese design.

It was the interior designers, however, who were the true keepers and innovators of tradition in Japanese design during the 1960s. Japanese fashion design established its position in the first half of the 1970s. Designer brand names that were specifically Japanese – Comme des Garçons and Issey Miyake, for example – were launched during this period and they called for the creation of special decors suited to their presentations.

The interior designers thus had very concrete tasks to accomplish, and they came up with revolutionary results. Since the 1970s in particular, they have re-interpreted the »primary structure« and »minimal art« style still inspired by traditional Japanese interior design, creating a form of expression that is distinctly Japanese. This is especially evident in Shigeru Uchida's early work of the 1970s. Form as such is neutralized in his designs; they do not seem to exist as concrete objects. At the same time, they are not removed from everyday life, from reality, but convey a unique and pulsating minimalism.

Since the 1980s, Japan has developed into an affluent consumer society, and the design created for it is more than functional; indeed, it is misused in a symbolic role that serves to highlight economic differences.

Cet ouvrage nous fait découvrir le «design japonais» actuel. La plupart des concepteurs présentés ici appartiennent au monde très actif du «Commercial and Interior Design», mais nous ferons également connaissance de designers d'avant-garde tels que Shiro Kuramata ou Shigeru Uchida. De par ses expressions très individualistes le design japonais a fait naître des œuvres surprenantes de nouveauté, qui ont enrichi le monde du stylisme bien au-delà du Japon.

Durant les années soixante, au Japon comme ailleurs, le Pop'Art a beaucoup influencé le design. Les dessins du groupe d'architectes anglais «Archigram» et le «Radical design» de groupes tels que «Archizoom», «Superstudio» ou «Global Tools» imprègnent encore le design japonais actuel.

Les «Interior Designers» ont récupéré l'héritage conceptuel de cette époque. Durant la première moitié des années soixante le monde japonais de la mode s'est construit une position autonome. Des noms bien japonais tels que «Comme des Garçons», Issey Miyake virent le jour et exigèrent des espaces particuliers pour présenter leurs créations.

Les stylistes d'intérieur, chargés de résoudre concrètement des problèmes, offrirent des solutions révolutionnaires. Bien qu'ils s'inspirent encore de la décoration intérieure japonaise traditionnelle, ils suggèrent, notamment depuis le début des années soixante-dix, une nouvelle interprétation de la «Primary Structure» et du «Minimal Art», créant ainsi une forme d'expression spécifique. Ceci se remarque particulièrement dans les premiers travaux de Shigeru Uchida réalisés à cette époque: la forme y est neutralisée en tant que telle et le sentiment de l'existence d'objets concrets disparaît, mais le quotidien et la réalité n'en sont pas exclus. On voit même s'y épanouir un minimalisme spécifique et plein de vie.

Depuis le début des années quatre-vingt le Japon devient une société de consommation où règne la surabondance, le design

schaft, und das Design wird mehr als funktionsbedingt eingesetzt, ja mißbraucht in einer symbolischen Rolle zur Hervorkehrung von wirtschaftlichen Unterschieden. In Zusammenhang mit diesem Kommerzialismus der achtziger Jahre muß der Entwerfer Naoki Sakai besonders erwähnt werden. Er trat in der Designwelt der achtziger Jahre nicht als herkömmlicher »Designer« auf, sondern bereits mit dem Titel eines »Konzeptors«. Auf der Bühne des Produktdesigns erhob er das Konzept nicht sichtbarer Waren zum Primat. Damit wurde das Konzept selbst zur Ware.

Läßt man so die Reihe der avantgardistischen Designer Japans vor seinem geistigen Auge auftreten, zeigen sich deutliche Charakteristika. Die Betätigungsfelder sind so weit verzweigt, daß man sie kaum unter den üblichen Bezeichnungen »Interior Designer« oder »Produktdesigner« zusammenfassen kann. Der echte Industriedesigner Masanori Umeda, der den ersten Braunpreis erhielt, hat sich später Memphis ergeben und seinen Stil von Grund auf gewandelt, ja sich sogar aktiv der »Shop-Interior-Design«-Szene bewegt. Der Designer Shiro Kuramata gestaltete Ende der achtziger Jahre viele Architekturprojekte. Seine Verdienste für die Welt des Interiordesigns sind groß, seine Haltung und seine Einstellung zur Raumgestaltung sind auch heute noch für viele seiner Anhänger richtungsweisend. Gerade seine Werke veranschaulichen deutlich, daß sich die Originalität des japanischen Designs allmählich zur vollen Blüte entfaltet. Dies kann nicht mit »traditionell japanisch« erklärt werden, sondern zeigt ein neues Japan, das sich selbstbewußt von der perfektionistischen Imitation westlicher Zivilisation gelöst hat.

Designer Naoki Sakai is especially noteworthy in connection with this commercialism of the 1980s. It was not as a »designer« in the conventional sense but as a self-styled »conceptor« that he first appeared on the design scene in the 1980s. In product design, he elevated the concept of non-visible goods to a principle of the highest order. Thus, the concept itself became a commodity.

In fact, if one allows one's eye to pass down the line of Japan's avant-garde designers, one finds a striking assortment of characteristics. Their fields of activity have branched out in so many directions that the usual headings of »interior designer« or »product designer« are hardly adequate to describe them. Masanori Umeda, a genuine industrial designer who was awarded the first Braun prize, later went over to Memphis and completely transformed his style. He even moved into the »shop interior design« scene. At the end of the 1980s, the designer Shiro Kuramata was the creator of many architectural projects. He has made major contributions to the world of interior design. His stance and approach to interior design are still regarded as trend-setting by many of his followers today. His work in particular clearly indicates that the originality of contemporary Japanese design is coming into its own. It is not merely a matter of recovering a »traditional Japanese« style. Rather, it is the manifestation of a new Japan, one which has finally broken away self-confidently from perfectionist imitations of Western culture.

devenant plus subordonné à la fonction; on l'exploite même en lui donnant un rôle symbolique qui révèle les différences économiques. Dans le contexte de cet esprit commercial le styliste Naoki Sakai mérite une mention particulière. Il ne fit pas son entrée dans le monde du design comme simple «designer», mais déjà comme «concepteur». Pour lui le concept des marchandises non visibles était primordial, et c'est ainsi que le concept lui-même devint marchandise. Si l'on dresse la liste des designers japonais d'avant-garde, on note des caractéristiques bien définies. Il est impossible de les regrouper sous les dénominations habituelles «designer d'intérieur» ou «designer de produit», car leurs champs d'activité sont trop divers. L'authentique designer industriel Masanori Umeda, qui reçut le premier prix Braun, s'est par la suite consacré à Memphis et a transformé son style du tout au tout, il a même collaboré activement au «shop interior design». Le designer Shiro Kuramata conçut vers la fin des années quatre-vingt de nombreux projets architectoniques. Le design d'intérieur lui doit beaucoup, ses idées sont encore révolutionnaires pour nombre de ses adeptes et l'originalité du design japonais s'épanouit dans ses travaux. L'expression «typiquement japonais» ne peut nous satisfaire: un Japon inconnu se révèle ici. Le Japon a trouvé son identité et cessé de reproduire parfaitement les créations de notre civilisation occidentale.

EINLEITUNG
Michael Mönninger

INTRODUCTION
Michael Mönninger

INTRODUCTION
Michael Mönninger

Der Schock

Von der prähistorischen Jomon-Keramik bis zu den zeitlosen Shoji-Papierwänden der Teehaus-Architektur hatte das japanische Design jahrhundertelang unverwechselbare Eigenschaften: das Bemühen um Praktikabilität und Funktionalität, ein tiefes Verständnis für natürliche Stoffe und ein sparsamer Umgang mit dem Material, größte handwerkliche Sorgfalt im Detail. Heute haben die Japaner eine neue Designgabe entwickelt. Vom Kapselhotel über tragbare Mini-Faxgeräte und Radio-Armbanduhren bis zur Video-Laser-Musicbox erfinden sie Dinge, von denen man sich nie hätte erträumen lassen, daß man sie brauchen könnte, aber die dank der Japaner zu einem nahezu unverzichtbaren Bestandteil unseres Alltags geworden sind.

Wer heute Japan besucht und die Idealvorstellungen der schweigsamen Ryoanji Steingärten und des asketischen Katsura Palastes von Kyoto im Kopf hat, trifft auf das schiere Gegenteil: eine hysterisch überkomplexe »consumer society«, in der die Moden und Konsumtrends scheinbar schneller wechseln als die Jahreszeiten.[1] Nirgendwo sonst auf der Erde gibt es eine derart vitale Massengesellschaft mit ähnlich unstillbaren Gelüsten. Schon das Bild der Metropolen im Städteband zwischen Tokio und Osaka strahlt das aus, was der Architekt Kazuo Shinohara die »Schönheit der progressiven Anarchie« nannte.[2] Die Städte sind steingewordene Chaos-Theorie und setzen sich nicht mehr aus Häusern und Straßen zusammen, sondern aus verkeilten Hauszwickeln und deformierten Resträumen, die keiner historischen Typologie mehr folgen. Nirgendwo gibt es eine solch rücksichtslose Ausbeutung des bewohnbaren Raumes, kein anderes Land hat dieses Maß an Fragmentierung, Überlagerung und Verdichtung erreicht. Das heutige Japan müßte man eher als eine »weiche« Struktur bezeichnen, in der die »Software« der Verkehrsströme und Menschenmassen,

The shock

From ancient Jomon ceramics to the timeless Shoji paper walls of tea-house architecture, Japanese design has seen many centuries of distinctive qualities: the striving after practicality and functionality, a profound grasp of natural materials coupled with their economical use, and the most meticulously detailed craftsmanship. In our own time, the Japanese have developed a new talent for design. From container hotels to portable mini-faxes to wristwatch radios to the video-laser musicbox, they have been inventing things no one would ever have dreamt they needed. And thanks to the Japanese they have become an essential part of our everyday life.

Those who visit Japan today with the silent Ryoanji rock gardens or the spartan palace of Katsura at Kyoto in mind are confronted with the complete opposite of their ideal notions: a frenetic, over-complex consumer society in which fashions and consumer trends change more rapidly than the seasons.[1] Nowhere else on earth is mass society so full of vitality, and so insatiable in its desires. The very image of the metropolises along the urban line from Tokyo to Osaka is one of what architect Kazuo Shinohara has called »the beauty of progressive anarchy«.[2] The cities are chaos theory in stone. They no longer consist of houses and streets, but rather of wedged-up slices of dwellings and deformed spatial scraps that are out of line with any and every historical type. Nowhere else is the land so ruthlessly exploited for building purposes. Nowhere else are things so fragmented, overlaid and compacted. Today's Japan ought best to be described as a »soft« structure in which the »software« – the traffic and the crowds, the information channels and sign

Sleep Capsule
Hotelcontainer, hotel compartment, conteneur-hôtel

Design Kisyio Kurokawa

Le choc

De la céramique préhistorique Jomon aux classiques murs de papier Shoji, le stylisme japonais a montré pendant des siècles des qualités incomparables, s'efforçant de rendre les objets pratiques et fonctionnels, manifestant une compréhension profonde pour les étoffes naturelles et utilisant les matériaux avec parcimonie et un grand souci de précision dans le détail. Aujourd'hui, les Japonais ont développé un nouveau don. Qu'il s'agisse des chambres d'hôtels-capsules ou des musicbox à lecture laser, sans oublier les fax miniature et les montres-radio, ils créent des choses dont nous n'aurions jamais songé avoir besoin, mais auxquelles nous ne pourrions renoncer aujourd'hui.

L'idéaliste qui se rend aujourd'hui au Japon avec, dans la tête, les silencieux jardins de pierre Ryoanji et l'ascétique Palais Katsura à Kyoto se retrouve confronté à la négation de tout cela, il découvre une société de consommation hystérique et ultracomplexe, dans laquelle les modes et les trends changent plus rapidement que les saisons.[1] Aucune autre société de par le monde ne manifeste une telle vitalité et une telle soif inextinguible de consommation. Déjà la métropole qui s'étire entre Tokyo et Osaka dégage cette «beauté de l'anarchie progressive», ainsi que la nomme l'architecte Kazuo Shinohara.[2] Les villes sont une théorie du chaos pétrifiée, elles ne se composent plus de bâtiments et de rues, mais de fragments coincés et d'espaces restants déformés, où on recherche vainement une typologie historique. Il n'existe nulle part ailleurs une telle exploitation abusive de l'espace habitable, aucun autre pays n'a poussé la fragmentation à ce point, n'a atteint un tel niveau de juxtaposition et de densification. Il faudrait plutôt définir le Japon actuel comme une structure «molle», dans laquelle le «logiciel» - les flux de circulation routière et les masses humaines, les canaux d'information et les

der Informationskanäle und Zeichensysteme über die »Hardware« von Architektur und Design dominiert.

Die jungen Menschen in Tokio leben nicht mehr in festen Häusern und Institutionen, sondern streifen wie Nomaden Tag und Nacht durch die Vergnügungszentren von Shinjuku, Shibuya, Akiharaba, Roppongi oder Akasaka. Sie versammeln sich an wechselnden Kulminationspunkten und kehren nur zum Schlafen und Kleiderwechseln in ihre winzigen Apartments zurück. Bislang galt das wilde Las Vegas als oberstes Sinnbild einer zügellos gewordenen Moderne. Doch gegenüber dem Lichterschein und dem Lärm im nächtlichen Tokio, das wie ein gigantischer Techno-Dancefloor vibriert, wirkt Las Vegas wie ein dämmriges Prärienest. Zwischen den Straßen ohne Namen und den Häusern ohne Fassaden verliert man jede Orientierung. Die Stadt wird überwuchert von einer unendlichen Fülle von Sekundär-Architekturen und Designs. Statt Gebäuden sieht man nur noch Symbole, Plakate, Neonzeichen, Straßenschilder, Reklametafeln, Warenauslagen, Wegweiser und Automaten, über denen wie eine Ersatznatur das undurchdringliche Metall-Efeu der oberirdisch verlegten Telefon- und Stromleitungen schwebt. Was Roland Barthes in seiner faszinierenden Tokio-Studie als das »Reich der Zeichen«[3] beschrieb, ist in Wahrheit der reine optische Overkill, ein brüllender Angriff auf das Auge, das nicht mehr liest, sondern die Umwelt wie ein Tastorgan haptisch erfaßt.

Westliche Beobachter zerbrechen sich schon seit längerem den Kopf, wie diese grelle Chaoswelt mit der Weltverneinung des Zen-Buddhismus und der Shinto-Religion des alten Japan zusammenpaßt. Wo ist die minimalistische Askese der traditionellen japanischen Ästhetik geblieben, die im 19. Jahrhundert noch die europäische Kunstrevolution des »Japonismus« ausgelöst hatte? Was ist aus jener klaren, naturalistisch-abstrahierenden Malerei und Grafik geworden, die auf die Moderne ähnlich wirkte wie die Wiederentdeckung der Antike auf die Renaissance?[4] Auch die Prediger und Apostel der Architektur- und Designmoderne, von Frank Lloyd Wright über Bruno Taut bis Charlotte Perriand, müßten in Japan heute andere Ideale suchen als die Pfosten- und Balkenkonstruktionen der alten Holzarchitektur oder die Schönheit der kargen Interieurs.

systems – predominate over the »hardware« of architecture and design.

Young people in Tokyo no longer live at fixed abodes or within defined institutions. They roam like nomads, by day and by night, through the entertainment districts of Shinjuku, Shibuya, Akiharaba, Roppongi or Akasaka. They gather at points where an intense buzz is reached, and return to their tiny apartments only to sleep and change their clothes. Hitherto, Las Vegas was considered the ultimate symbol of unbridled modern life. But Las Vegas is a sleepy prairie nowhere, compared with the lights and the noise of nighttime Tokyo, vibrant as some gigantic techno dancefloor. In amongst the nameless streets and faceless houses, you lose your bearings entirely. An infinite proliferation of secondary architecture and designs is overgrowing the city. Instead of buildings, all you see are symbols, posters, neon signs, street signs, advertisements, displays of goods, direction signs and automats. Above it all, like some ersatz Nature, hangs the impenetrable metal ivy of overground telephone and electricity cables. In his fascinating study of Tokyo, Roland Barthes spoke of the »empire of signs«;[3] in truth it is pure optical overkill, a shrill assault on the eye, which no longer reads but rather experiences the environment palpably, as if by touch.

For some time, Western observers have been wondering how this loud, chaotic world can possibly fit together with the traditional Zen Buddhist abnegation of the world and with old Japan's Shinto religion. What became of the ascetic minimalism of traditional Japanese aesthetics, which prompted the 19th-century artistic reorientation in Europe known as japonisme? What became of the lucid painting and graphic art, naturalistic yet abstract, that had an impact on Modernist art comparable with that of the rediscovery of antiquity on the Renaissance?[4] The preachers and disciples of Modernism in architecture and design, from Frank Lloyd Wright to Bruno Taut to Charlotte Perriand, would nowadays have to seek quite other ideals in Japan than the post-and-beam construction of olden wooden architecture or the beauty of spartan interiors.

Hitherto, the beauty of Japan was primarily in the eye of the Western beholder. For a full hundred years, the European longing

systèmes sémiotiques - prendrait le pas sur le «matériel» que représentent l'architecture et le design.

A Tokyo, les jeunes gens ne vivent plus dans des constructions fixes et des institutions, mais errent jour et nuit dans les centres de divertissement de Shinjuku, Shibuya, Akiharaba, Roppongi ou Akasaka. Ils se rassemblent à différents points chauds, et ne se rendent dans leurs appartements minuscules que pour dormir ou se changer. C'est Las Vegas qui était jusqu'ici le symbole d'une modernité déchaînée. Mais comparée au Tokyo nocturne, ses lumières et ses bruits, ses vibrations qui la transforment en une gigantesque piste de danse technicisée, Las Vegas n'est plus qu'un trou obscur perdu dans la prairie. Les rues sans nom et les maisons sans façade font perdre tout sens de l'orientation. Les architectures et stylismes secondaires pullulent et envahissent la ville. Au lieu de bâtiments on ne voit plus que des symboles, des affiches, des néons, des plaques de rues, de la réclame, des étalages de marchandises, des panneaux indicateurs et des jeux automatiques au-dessus desquels, tel un succédané de nature, plane le lierre métallique et impénétrable des câbles de téléphone et d'électricité. Ce que Roland Barthes décrivait comme le «Royaume des signes»[3] dans son étude fascinante sur Tokyo est en réalité un véritable overkill optique; l'œil est violemment attaqué, il ne lit plus, mais perçoit son environnement en le palpant comme le fait un organe tactile.

Les observateurs occidentaux cherchent encore à comprendre comment ce monde criard et chaotique est compatible avec la négation du monde que prône le bouddhisme zen ou la religion shinto de l'ancien Japon. Où est passé le dépouillement caractéristique de l'esthétique traditionnelle japonaise qui avait au 19ème siècle déclenché la révolution artistique du japonisme en Europe? Que sont devenus ces peintures et ces graphismes clairs, à mi-chemin entre le naturalisme et l'abstraction, qui ont eu sur les temps modernes la même influence que l'Antiquité pour les contemporains de la Renaissance?[4] Même les prédicateurs et les apôtres de l'architecture et du design modernes, de Frank Lloyd Wright à Charlotte Perriand en passant par Bruno Taut, devraient aujourd'hui chercher au Japon d'autres idéaux que les anciennes constructions de bois ou la beauté des sobres intérieurs.

Die Schönheit Japans lag bislang vor allem im Auge des westlichen Betrachters. Europas Sehnsucht nach Japan war seit hundert Jahren von einer Suche nach primitivistischen Urbildern geprägt, um den zivilisatorischen Zumutungen des Westens zu entfliehen. Wie Anfang des Jahrhunderts die Bildhauer die Negerplastik, die Maler die Südsee, die Dadaisten die Kindersprache und die Psychologen das archaische Unbewußte entdeckten, so war Japan für Architekten und Designer das Land der »edlen Zen-Armut, die helfen möge, verlorene Werte wieder zu etablieren und unsere Augen (zu) öffnen für Erfahrungen, die unserem Leben abgehen«, so Walter Gropius.[5]

Diese Tradition der Einfachheit und Elementarität scheint heute wie weggewischt. Natürlich findet man noch Tatami-Matten und rituelles No-Theater, aber wer heute einen jungen Japaner fragt, wo man einer richtigen Teezeremonie mit furo-Kohlebecken samt gotoku-Aufsatz, mit kenzui- und mizusashi-Wasserbehältern und kama-Kessel beiwohnen könne, um das heilige Heißgetränk aus echten chawan-Schalen zu genießen, muß damit rechnen, ins nächste Volkskundemuseum verwiesen zu werden. Dennoch kann auch das moderne Japan helfen, westliche Augen für unbekannte Erfahrungen zu öffnen. Und trotz aller Internationalisierung hat das Land gewisse Elemente der traditionellen Ästhetik bewahrt, wenngleich sie unendlich transformiert und abstrahiert wurden. Dafür muß man allerdings den Formbegriff Ästhetik in seiner umfassenderen Urbedeutung als »sinnliche Wahrnehmung« verstehen. Damit ist nicht bloß die objektbezogene Formenwahl und Gestaltung von Gegenständen gemeint, sondern auch ihre subjektbezogenen Anmutungs- und Aneignungsqualitäten, ihre praktische Doppeldeutigkeit und, fast könnte man sagen, ihre spirituelle Spannung.

»Furoshikibility«

»Furoshiki« zum Beispiel. Furoshiki ist ein einfaches Stück Stoff, mit dem man alles verpacken kann, gleichgültig, ob Geldscheine, Gemüse oder Bücher. Furoshiki ist ein äußerst vielseitiges Tragegerät, das man nach dem Gebrauch zusammenfaltet und in die Tasche steckt. Der japanische Designer Kenji Ekuan, Jahrgang 1929, hat am

for Japan was marked by the quest for primitivist sources. The West, felt to be over-civilized, was becoming difficult to endure. Just as, at the beginning of the century, sculptors discovered the sculptural work of black peoples, painters the South Seas, Dadaists the language of children, and psychologists the archaic unconscious, so too Japan – in the eyes of architects and designers – became the land of »that noble poverty of Zen, which may help to reestablish lost values and open our eyes for experiences that are absent from our lives«, as Walter Gropius put it.[5]

This tradition of the simple and basic now seems to have been swept away. Of course there are still Tatami mats and the ritual Noh theatre. But if you ask a young Japanese where you can witness an authentic tea ceremony with a furo charcoal bowl complete with gotoku top, kenzui and mizusashi water vessels and a kama kettle, and genuine chawan bowls from which to imbibe the sacred hot beverage, you may well be sent to the nearest ethnological museum. And yet even modern Japan can open Western eyes to experiences hitherto unknown. Despite the internationalization of the country, it has retained certain elements of its traditional aesthetics, albeit in an immeasurably transformed and abstracted mode. In saying this, of course, we must take the term »aesthetics« in its broader etymological connotation of »sense perception« – concerning not only the objective choice of form and shaping of an item, but also this item's subjective qualities of appearance and implication, their practical ambiguity, and what we might almost term their spiritual tension.

»Furoshikibility«

Take »Furoshiki«, for instance. Furoshiki is a simple piece of material that can be used for wrapping anything: banknotes, vegetables, books. Furoshiki is an extremely versatile carrier that can be folded up after use and popped in your pocket. The Japanese designer Kenji Ekuan (born 1929) took the Furoshiki as a way of elucidating oriental thinking on design. Western carriers are of a design specifically matched to their purpose: a wallet for money, a special bookbag, a net for vegetables. For this reason, the West has many things of a monofunctional nature, whereas the Japanese prefer

Jusqu'ici, c'est surtout la manière de voir du spectateur occidental qui faisait la beauté du Japon. La nostalgie qu'éprouvait l'Europe envers ce pays était marquée depuis un siècle par une recherche d'archétypes primitifs, cherchant à fuir les exigences civilisatrices de l'Occident. Tout comme au début du siècle les sculpteurs découvrirent les plastiques nègres, les peintres les mers du Sud, les dadaïstes le langage infantile et les psychologues l'inconscient archaïque, le Japon devint pour les architectes et les stylistes le pays de la «noble pauvreté zen qui pourrait nous aider à rétablir des valeurs perdues et à nous rendre accessibles des expériences qui nous demeurent fermées», selon Walter Gropius.[5]

Cette sobriété et ce dépouillement traditionnels semblent disparus. Evidemment, les tatamis et le théâtre No existent encore, mais demander à un jeune Japonais où l'on peut assister à une vraie cérémonie du thé avec un réchaud furo et son gotoku, avec les kenzui et mizusashi pour l'eau et la bouilloire kama, et boire le breuvage sacré dans de vraies coupes chawan, c'est s'exposer à se retrouver dans un musée ethnologique. Pourtant, le Japon moderne peut aussi aider les Occidentaux à ouvrir les yeux sur l'inconnu. Et malgré l'internationalisation, le pays a gardé certains éléments de l'esthétique traditionnelle, même si ceux-ci ont été infiniment transformés et abstraits. Mais pour cela, il faut comprendre le concept formel «esthétique» dans sa signification originelle plus vaste, sa racine étant «sentir». Il ne s'agit pas seulement ici de critères relatifs à l'objet, au choix de la forme et de la mise en forme, mais aussi de critères relatifs au sujet, à l'impression que lui laisse l'objet, à l'assimilation qui se produit, à la double signification pratique des objets et, est-on tenté de dire, à leur tension spirituelle.

La «furoshikibilité»

Prenons par exemple furoshiki: c'est un morceau de tissu dans lequel on peut emballer et transporter ce que l'on veut, des billets de banque, des légumes ou des livres. Furoshiki est un accessoire polyvalent, que l'on replie après usage, et que l'on glisse dans sa poche. Le styliste japonais Kenji Ekuan, né en 1929, a expliqué la conception stylistique de l'Extrême-Orient à l'aide de furoshiki. En Occident, l'accessoire

Beispiel des Furoshiki das fernöstliche Design-Denken erläutert. Westliche Transportgeräte seien gebrauchsspezifisch; eine Brieftasche sei eigens für Geld, eine Tasche für Bücher und ein Netz für Gemüse konstruiert. Deshalb gebe es im Westen unendlich viele monofunktionale Dinge, während sich Japaner lieber mit nur wenigen Mehrzweckgeräten umgäben. »Das westliche zweckspezifische Werkzeug wurde für eine bestimmte Aufgabe gestaltet, und jeder, der das richtige Werkzeug benutzt, wird vermutlich dieselben Resultate erzielen. Das traditionelle japanische Mehrzweckwerkzeug verlangt durch seine Vielseitigkeit größere Kreativität und Begabung seines Benutzers. Man könnte das westliche Werkzeug hardware-ähnlich nennen und das japanische software-ähnlich. Das eine ist eine mechanische Apparatur, die einen bestimmten Zweck bedient, aber auf diesen beschränkt ist, während das andere größere Ansprüche an seinen Benutzer stellt, sich aber mit der menschlichen Vorstellungskraft in seiner Funktionalität erweitern läßt.«[6]

Ekuans »Furoshikibility« läßt sich in zahlreichen japanischen Gebrauchsgegenständen wiederfinden. So wie die papiernen Shoji-Schiebewände zugleich Fenster und Gardine sind, so lassen sich die primitiven Eßstäbchen als Kombination von Messer und Gabel ansehen, die zugleich das Auflegen, Zertrennen und Essen erlauben. Die Mehrfachfunktion des Tatami-Strohfußbodens als Geh-, Sitz-, Liege- und Schlaffläche war übrigens ein ganz banaler Grund für die überaus sparsame Möblierung der alten Häuser, die weder Stuhl, Bett noch Sofa brauchten. Auch die Räume dienten nicht einem bestimmten Zweck, sondern ließen sich mittels Schiebetüren tagsüber zum Wohnzimmer und nachts zum Schlafgemach umwandeln.

Von dieser aus Armut geborenen, phantasievollen Einfachheit und Vieldeutigkeit den Bogen zur heutigen »consumer society« zu schlagen erscheint gewagt. Aber steckt nicht im Kern derselbe Denkansatz darin, wenn japanische Firmen heute lieber mit der Marketing-Schrotflinte schießen und alles direkt auf den Markt bringen, während westliche Fabrikanten zielgenau auf Konsumentenschichten hinarbeiten und ihre Produkte jahrelang testen und verbessern? Jährlich kreieren beispielsweise japanische Limonadefabriken eintausend

to have only a few, multifunctional things. »The Western tool is made for a specific purpose, and anyone who uses the proper tool will presumably achieve the same results. The traditional Japanese multi-purpose tool demands, by its sheer versatility, greater creativity and aptitude on the part of the user. One might say that the Western tool is like hardware and the Japanese like software. The one is a mechanical implement that serves a particular purpose but no more than that one purpose, while the other makes greater demands of its user but is capable of an infinite extension of its possible functions according to the powers of the human imagination«.[6]

Ekuan's »Furoshikibility« can be seen in numerous Japanese utility objects. Just as paper Shoji sliding walls are a combination of window and curtain, so too chopsticks, rudimentary as they are, can be seen as a combination of knife and fork that can be used for serving food, separating it, and raising it to the mouth. The multi-function of Tatami straw floor covering as a place to walk, sit, lie or sleep constituted a straight-forward reason why old-style homes were so very sparsely furnished, with neither chairs, nor beds, nor settees. Nor did the rooms themselves serve any defined purpose. Instead, the sliding doors could be used to make them living rooms by day and bedrooms by night.

It may seem a bold step to associate this imaginative simplicity and versatility, born of poverty, with today's consumer society. But if Japanese companies spray their marketing grapeshot, firing all they have at the market right away, while Western manufacturers target specific strata of consumers, testing and improving their products over decades, can we not detect the same thinking at the heart of this difference? Every year, to take just one example, Japanese lemonade manufacturers come up with a thousand new soft drinks, 99% of which promptly sink back into oblivion. But the remaining one per cent enjoys high market sales.[7] The possible take-up is tried out, rather than being laboriously planned. Games-playing and bricolage are ranked higher than rationalist concepts. If Sony

Urushi, 1986
Schale, bowl, coupe

Design Toshiyuki Kita

en question dépend de ce qu'il est censé transporter: l'argent va dans le portefeuille, les livres dans le sac et les légumes dans un filet. Et c'est pour cette raison qu'il existe autant d'objets monovalents chez nous, alors que les Japonais préfèrent s'entourer d'objets polyvalents en moindre nombre. »L'outil occidental à objectif spécifique a été créé pour une tâche particulière, et tous ceux qui utiliseront l'outil adéquat, obtiendront probablement les mêmes résultats. Le traditionnel outil japonais polyvalent réclame de par sa complexité un utilisateur plus créatif et plus doué. On pourrait dire que notre outil occidental est semblable au «matériel» et le japonais au «logiciel». Le premier est purement mécanique et n'obéit qu'à un objectif particulier, ce qui limite ses fonctions, alors que l'autre demande plus à son utilisateur, mais que la gamme de ses fonctions dépend de l'imagination humaine».[6]

On retrouve la thèse de Ekuan dans de nombreux objets utilitaires japonais. Les panneaux de papier shoji sont à la fois fenêtres et rideaux, les baguettes primitives sont à la fois couteaux et fourchettes répartissant et poussant la nourriture. On peut marcher, s'asseoir, se coucher et dormir sur les nattes tatami, et c'est pour cette raison, banale en soi, que les anciennes maisons avaient si peu de meubles: on n'avait besoin ni de chaises, ni de lits, ni de canapés. Et les pièces n'avaient pas non plus de rôle spécifique: la salle de séjour se transformait la nuit en chambre à coucher grâce aux portes coulissantes.

Il semble osé de faire un rapprochement entre cette simplicité cachant des possibilités multiples et la société de consommation actuelle. Mais ne retrouve-t-on pas cette idée dans la méthode de marketing «criblante» des entreprises japonaises actuelles qui mettent tout directement sur le marché, alors que les fabricants occidentaux travaillent pour des groupes-cibles, testant et améliorant leurs produits pendant des années? On sait que les fabricants de limonade japonais créent chaque année mille nouvelles boissons, 99 pour cent d'entre elles disparaîtront à nouveau mais on s'arrachera le dernier pour cent.[7] L'essai prédomine sur la planification méticuleuse. Le jeu et le «bricolage» ont plus de valeur que les concepts rationalistes. Sony sort actuellement mille appareils chaque année - 800 sont des améliorations et 200 con-

neue Softdrinks, von denen 99 Prozent wieder in der Versenkung verschwinden, während das verbleibende eine Prozent dann zum Umsatzrenner wird.[7] Man probiert die Verwendungsfähigkeit aus, anstatt sie umständlich zu planen. Spiel und »bricolage« haben einen höheren Stellenwert als rationalistische Konzepte. Wenn Sony heute jedes Jahr tausend neue Geräte herausbringt – achthundert davon sind Verbesserungen, zweihundert schaffen wirklich neue Märkte –, dann sind diese endlosen Warenkolonnen nichts anderes als immer neue Variationen darüber, wie multiple Zwecke sich ihre stets wandelnden Mittel suchen.[8]

Die Wirtschaftsmacht

Nur mit dem Denkkonzept von Eßstäbchen und Bodenmatten allein wäre Japan allerdings kaum zur Industriemacht geworden. Bei aller Vorliebe für folkloristische Erklärungen müssen Westler erkennen, daß die Japaner mit ihrer Gabe zur Imitation und Perfektionierung teilweise noch westlicher denken und arbeiten als sie selbst. Noch gut in Erinnerung ist die Zeit nach dem Zweiten Weltkrieg, als der Inselstaat der größte Raubkopierer der Welt war. Vor allem amerikanische Firmen beschwerten sich in den fünfziger Jahren bei der japanischen Regierung über die dreisten Beutezüge japanischer Firmen. 1958 gründete deshalb das sagenumwobene »Ministry of International Trade and Industry« (MITI) eine eigene Gesellschaft zur Designförderung, die »Japan Industrial Design Promotion Organization« (JIDPO). Jährlich wurde ausgewählten neuen Produkten das »G-Prädikat für gutes Design und wahre Originalität« verliehen, um das Abkupfern zu ächten. Damals kam Sony auf die Idee, erstmals Transistoren, die die Amerikaner zwar erfunden hatten, aber nur zum Bau von Hörgeräten verwendeten, in das weltweit erste kleine Transistorradio »Type 63« von 1957 einzubauen. 1959 kam Sonys erstes volltransistoriertes TV-Portable heraus, und seitdem hat die Sturzflut japanischer Erfindungen bis hin zum handteller-großen Camcorder von Matsushita und Sony 1987 nicht mehr aufgehört.

Anfangs hatte sich das heute zwölftausend Mitarbeiter starke MITI noch auf die Förderung von Schwerindustrie, Schiffs- und Automobilbau konzentriert. Doch seitdem die

produces a thousand new gadgets a year – eight hundred of them being improved versions and the other two hundred genuinely creating new markets – these unending droves of goods represent no more than ever-new variations on the quest of multifunctionalism for its ever-changing vehicles.[8]

Economic Power

If Japan had had no more than the concepts of chopsticks and floor matting to offer, the country would of course never have become an industrial power. Much as they might like their folksy explanations, it is important that Westerners grasp the fact that the Japanese gift for imitating and perfecting partly outdoes the West at its own ways of think-ing and working. The period after the Second World War, when the island realm was the world's greatest thief and copycat, remains unforgotten. American companies in particular complained to the Japanese government in the 1950s about the blatant industrial pillaging in which Japanese were indulgeing. In 1958 the legendary Ministry of International Trade and Industry (MITI) founded its own association to promote design, the Japan Industrial Design Promotion Organization (JIDPO). Every year, selected new products were given the G Award for Good Design and Genuine Originality – a step towards stopping copycatting. It was then that Sony hit on the idea of building transistors (which the Americans had invented but were using only in hearing-aids) into the first ever transistor radio, the 1957 Type 63. In 1959 Sony produced their first fully transistorized portable TV. Since then, the tidal wave of Japanese inventions, through to the palmsized Camcorder made by Matsushita and Sony in 1987, has been unstoppable.

At first MITI, which now employs 12,000 people, concentrated on fostering heavy industry, shipbuilding and car manufacturing. But once the Asian tigers – Hong Kong, Singapore, Korea and Taiwan – and then the cheap labour nations from the Philippines to China emerged as serious competitors for the Japanese, economical mass production ceased to represent an effective competition advantage. Speeding up technological development, and quality control, became paramount once it was no

quièrent vraiment de nouveaux marchés -, et ils ne sont rien d'autre que de nouvelles variations sur le thème des fins multiples dans leur quête de moyens toujours en évolution.[8]

La puissance économique

Mais ce ne sont pas les baguettes et les tatamis qui ont fait du Japon une puissance industrielle. Même si les Occidentaux ont un faible pour les explications folkoriques, ils doivent reconnaître que les Japonais doués pour l'imitation et le perfectionnement pensent et travaillent parfois de manière plus occidentale qu'eux. L'époque où les Japonais étaient les plus grands plagiaires du monde, après la Seconde Guerre mondiale, est restée dans les mémoires. Dans les années 50, les sociétés américaines s'en plaignirent d'ailleurs auprès du gouvernement japonais. Le célèbre «Ministry of International Trade and Industry» (MITI) fonda pour cette raison en 1958 sa propre société de promotion du design, la «Japan Industrial Design Promotion Organization» (JIDPO). Pour mettre fin à cette piraterie organisée, le «Prix G pour un design réussi et une réelle originalité» était attribué tous les ans à de nouveaux produits sélectionnés. C'est à cette époque que Sony eut l'idée de placer des transistors, que les Américains avaient inventés mais n'utilisaient que dans dans les prothèses auditives, dans la plus petite radio du monde, le «type 63» de 1957. En 1959, Sony sortit la première télévision portable complètement transistorisée, et depuis le flux des inventions japonaises n'a pas tari; en 1987, Matsushita et Sony ont présenté le camcorder, grand comme la paume de la main.

Au départ, la MITI, qui emploie 12.000 personnes aujourd'hui, avait concentré ses efforts sur la promotion de l'industrie lourde, la construction navale et automobile. Mais depuis que la Corée, Formose, Hongkong et Singapour, et surtout depuis que les nouveaux pays aux bas salaires tels que les Philippines et la Chine sont devenus des concurrents dangereux, la production de masse à bon marché n'est plus un avantage au niveau de la compétition. Depuis que ce n'est plus le prix mais la technique et la forme qui garantissent le succès japonais, l'accélération de l'évolution technologique et le contrôle de la qualité sont deve-

asiatischen Tiger – Korea, Taiwan, Hong-kong und Singapur und besonders die neuen Billiglohnländer von den Philippinen bis China – den Japanern schärfste Konkurrenz machten, ist die kostengünstige Massenfertigung kein Wettbewerbsvorteil mehr. Die Beschleunigung der technologischen Entwicklung und die Qualitätskontrolle wurden zum obersten Staatsziel, seitdem nicht mehr der Preis, sondern die technische und formale Gestaltung den japanischen Erfolg garantiert. 1989 verkündete die Regierung ein »Design-Jahr«, veranstaltete vierhundert Workshops und Kolloquien und gründete Designzentren in allen Präfekturen, um das Land für den postindustriellen Exportkampf zu rüsten.[9]

Typisch japanisch?

Die spezifisch japanische Note im Design der weltweit erfolgreichen Motorräder von Yamaha, Honda, Suzuki und Kawasaki läßt sich ebensoschwer festmachen wie die ostasiatische Besonderheit in der Gestaltung von Sony-Fernsehern, Canon-Cameras oder Sharp-Taschenrechnern. Die Frage nach den kulturellen Wurzeln dieser Exportschlager geht reichlich fehl, weil es Produkte eines globalen Designs sind, das nationale und mentale Grenzen längst übersprungen hat. Japanisches Design heißt nicht, daß das edle, graue, wildlederartige Finish von Yamaha- oder Sony-Hifigeräten an die ernsten, düsteren Farben der Malerei aus der Edo-Periode erinnert. Der Begriff japanisches Design zielt vielmehr auf eine bestimmte Kategorie von Produkten. Globales Technik- und Elektronik-Design ist japanisch, genau so, wie globales Filmdesign aus Hollywood kommt oder globale Luxuswaren von französischen Couturiers und Juwelieren stammen.
Solche Klischees sind in Japan ebenso wirksam wie wirklichkeitsnah. Denn neunzig Prozent der japanischen Designer sind keine Künstlerindividuen, sondern arbeiten als Angestellte von großen Konzernen. Für Design und Produktentwicklung beschäftigt Sharp zweihundert Mitarbeiter, Panasonic fünfhundert, Toyota sechshundert und Sony (einschließlich Grafik) sogar zweitausendfünfhundert. Bahnbrechende Designerstars wie Nigel Coates oder Philippe Starck gibt es in Japan kaum, weil exzessiver Individualismus verpönt ist. Darin könnte man sogar Nachwirkungen der für den

longer the price but technical and formal qualities that underwrote Japanese success. In 1989 the government called a »Design Year«, holding some 400 workshops and symposiums and establishing design centres in all the country's prefectures, to gird up the nation for the post-industrial export battle.[9]

Typically Japanese?

It is as difficult to say what is distinctively Japanese in the globally top-ranking Yamaha, Honda, Suzuki and Kawasaki motorbikes as it is to make out a peculiarly Far Eastern component in Sony televisions, Canon cameras or Sharp calculators. To enquire after the cultural roots of these export winners is pointless. They are products of a global design thinking which has long since crossed the borders, both national and mental. To speak of Japanese design is not to suggest that the austere grey leathery finish of Yamaha or Sony hifi systems recalls the dark and sombre colours of Edo period painting, say. Rather, the concept of Japanese design aims at a particular class of products. Technological and electronic design worldwide is Japanese, just as film design worldwide derives from Hollywood or luxury goods from French couturiers and jewellers.
Clichés of this order are tellingly apt in Japan, for 90 per cent of Japanese designers are not artists in their own individual right but employees of large firms. In their design and product development departments, Sharp employ 200, Panasonic 500, Toyota 600 and Sony (including graphics) an impressive 2,500. Pioneering star designers such as Nigel Coates or Philippe Starck are almost unknown in Japan, since excessive individualism is frowned upon. In this, we might detect the aftereffects of Zen Buddhism's emphasis on abstractive reduction and anonymity, and on the supreme importance of »eradicating all trace of individual origin«.[10] The three prime hallmarks of Japanese industrial design – simplicity, compactness and precision in detail – are in the Bauhaus, Braun and Bang & Olufsen tradition, but at the same time go well beyond it. In Europe, form and casing are of more importance than detail, whereas in the Japanese aesthetic of »modular character« the multiplication of specific small units »proceeds from interior

nus les objectifs primaires de l'Etat. En 1989, le gouvernement a annoncé une «année du design», il a organisé 400 workshops et conférences et fondé des centres de design dans toutes les circonscriptions afin de préparer le pays à la lutte pour l'exportation qui suivra l'ère industrielle.[9]

Typiquement japonais?

Le trait typiquement japonais se laisse aussi difficilement déceler dans le style des célèbres motos Yamaha, Honda, Suzuki et Kawasaki que dans les formes des téléviseurs Sony, des caméras Canon et des calculatrices Sharp. Il serait vain de rechercher les racines de ces bestsellers, vu que nous avons affaire ici aux produits d'un design global ayant fait sauter depuis longtemps les frontières nationales et mentales. La notion de design japonais ne signifie pas que le finish noble, gris, suédé des appareils Hifi de Yamaha ou Sony évoque les couleurs sévères et grises de la peinture de la période de Edo. Ce qu'on entend par design japonais concerne bien davantage une catégorie déterminée de produits. Le design technique et électronique global est japonais, tout comme le design cinématographique global vient de Hollywood, et que la haute couture et les bijoux de luxe sont des produits français.
Au Japon, de tels clichés sont aussi efficaces que proches de la réalité. Car 90 pour cent des stylistes japonais ne sont pas des artistes solitaires, mais travaillent pour de grands groupes industriels. Sharp emploie deux cents personnes dans son département Design et Développement, Panasonic cinq cents, Toyota six cents et Sony même deux mille cinq cents (dessinateurs techniques inclus). Le Japon, qui réprouve l'individualisme excessif, ne compte guère de vedettes du format de Nigel Coates ou Philippe Starck. On serait tenté d'y voir les répercussions de la philosophie zen qui cherche à atteindre l'abstraction et l'anonymat, et dont l'objectif principal est d' «effacer les traces de l'élévation individuelle».[10] Les trois caractéristiques principales du design industriel japonais – la simplicité, la compacité et la précision dans le détail – ont absorbé la tradition du Bauhaus, de Braun et Bang & Olufsen, mais elles vont beaucoup plus loin que cela. En Europe, les formes et le contenant ont la primauté sur

Zen-Buddhismus charakteristischen abstrahierenden Reduktion und Anonymität sehen, für die stets das »Löschen der Spuren der individuellen Hervorbringung« oberstes Ziel war.[10] Die drei Hauptmerkmale des japanischen Industriedesigns – Einfachheit, Kompaktheit und Detailgenauigkeit – haben zwar die Bauhaus-, Braun- und Bang & Olufsen-Tradition aufgenommen, reichen aber weit darüber hinaus. In Europa geht die Form und das Gehäuse über das Detail, während in der japanischen Ästhetik der »Modular-Charakter«, die Multiplikation von spezifischen kleinen Maßeinheiten »von innen nach außen schreitet, vom Detail zum Ganzen, vom Mikro- zum Makroskopischen«.[11]

Die Schwierigkeit, das japanische Formgefühl zu verstehen, rührt von der andersartigen Raumauffassung her. Westliche Augen sind gewöhnt, den Raum in einheitlichen geometrischen Grundformen wahrzunehmen. Der Raum kulminiert stets in einem subjektabhängigen zentralperspektivischen Fluchtpunkt. Das japanische Konzept des Zwischenraumes dagegen meint ein gleichzeitig räumliches und zeitliches Intervall in der Wahrnehmung von Gegenständen. Dazwischen herrscht nicht bloß Leere, sondern etwas Eigenständiges, ein objektives Spannungsverhältnis – vergleichbar mit einer musikalischen Pause. Und weil Spannung nie aus Symmetrie, sondern nur aus heterogenen Elementen entstehen kann, gibt es in der traditionellen Gestaltung weder Zentralität noch Spiegelbildlichkeit. Selbst der Katsura Palast, eine Kultstätte für die Architekturmoderne, weist trotz seiner strengen Form keine Symmetrie auf.

Die Vermutung, die japanische Gabe zur Minimierung und Miniaturisierung rühre davon her, daß Japaner durchschnittlich zehn Zentimeter kleiner als Europäer sind, sei hier nur zur Belustigung erwähnt.[12] Eher sind der enorme Druck des Stadtlebens und die aus Kostengründen minimierten Wohnungen mit ihrem winzigen Stauraum der Grund, daß der Entwurf von Architektur und Design zu einer fast moralischen Aufgabe wird, weil Raum unbezahlbar teuer ist.

Der Architekt Yoshinobu Ashihara erklärt die japanische Detailsorgfalt damit, daß Räume und Gegenstände stets »zentrifugal konzipiert werden, indem sie von innen heraus durch Addition« entstehen – im Gegensatz zur »zentripetalen Gestaltung mit-

to exterior, from part to whole, from microscopic to macroscopic«.[11]

Difficulties in grasping the Japanese sense of form originate in the different conception of space. Western eyes are accustomed to perceiving space in unified and defined geometrical shapes. Space is seen as receding to a vanishing point in a central perspective dependent on the perceiving subject. The Japanese concept of intermediate space, by contrast, signifies a hiatus (in terms of both time and space) in the perception of objects. Between them, there is not mere vacancy, but rather a discrete phenomenon, an objective state of tension - comparable with a musical rest. And, since tension can never result from symmetry, only from heterogeneity, there is neither centrality nor mirror-image reflection in traditional design. Even the Katsura Palace, a cult site for modern architecture, is innocent of symmetry, for all its formal austerity.

The notion that the Japanese talent for minimization and miniaturization derives from the fact that the Japanese are on average ten centimetres shorter than Europeans need be mentioned here only as a humorous aside.[12] More plausible causes are the immense pressure of city life and the cost-related minimization of living space: architecture and design have acquired an almost moral dimension, because, quite simply, no one can afford space any more.

The architect Yoshinobu Ashihara has an explanation for the Japanese meticulousness over detail. He believes that rooms and objects are always »conceived centrifugally, created from within outwards, additively« – in contrast to the »centripetal creative principle, using subtraction« that applies in the West.[13] Ashihara compares the Japanese approach with the making of clay sculpture: the parts of the whole are added bit by bit. The Western approach, on the other hand, is that of a sculptor who chisels away at a block of stone, gradually revealing the parts from out of the whole. This renders comprehensible the sheer chaos of Japanese cities, and the total absence of any overall plan or figuration,

Primitive Android
Fernsehgerät, television set, appareil de télévision
Design Shozo Toyohisa

le détail, alors que pour l'esthétisme japonais le «caractère modulaire», la multiplication de petites unités de mesure spécifiques, se déplace de «l'intérieur vers l'extérieur, du détail à l'ensemble, du microscopique au macroscopique».[11]

Les difficultés que nous éprouvons à comprendre le sentiment de la forme japonais repose sur une conception différente de l'espace. Pour les yeux occidentaux, l'espace est perçu en tant que formes de base géométriques homogènes. Il culmine toujours dans un point de fuite central et dépendant du sujet. Pour les Japonais, il existe par contre un intervalle spatial aussi bien que temporel dans la perception des objets. Ici, il n'y a pas de vide entre les objets, mais quelque chose d'autonome, une relation de tension subjective - comparable à une pause musicale. Et comme la tension ne peut jamais naître de la symétrie, mais uniquement d'éléments hétérogènes, la mise en forme traditionnelle ne conçoit ni centralité ni correspondance autour d'un axe. On cherchera vainement une symétrie quelconque dans les formes sévères du Palais Katsura, qui est pourtant un monument de l'architecture moderne.

On a même supposé, amusons-nous un peu,[12] que c'est la petite taille des Japonais, ils ont en moyenne dix centimètres de moins que les Européens, qui les rend si doués pour la réduction et la miniaturisation. La raison pour laquelle l'architecture et le stylisme deviennent presque un devoir moral serait plutôt à rechercher dans l'énorme pression due à la vie urbaine et aux logements minuscules, car l'espace est incroyablement cher.

L'architecte Yoshinobu Ashihara explique que la minutie japonaise repose sur le fait que les espaces et les objets sont toujours «conçus de manière centrifuge, ils sont créés par addition en partant de l'intérieur» contrairement à la «réalisation centripète par la soustraction» que pratiquent les Occidentaux.[13] Ashihara emploie l'image suivante pour comparer les deux manières de procéder: le Japonais modèle la glaise et rajoute celle-ci petit à petit, alors que l'Occidental travaille à partir d'un bloc de pierre qu'il dégrossit peu à peu. On comprend dès lors le chaos qui règne dans les métropoles japonaises et l'absence complète de supervision d'ensemble, ce qui fait frémir d'horreur les Européens. Ici, les parties dominent le Tout. La maison particulière

tels Subtraktion« im Westen.[13] Ashihara vergleicht die japanische Herangehensweise mit der Erschaffung einer Lehmskulptur, an die Stück für Stück dem Ganzen hinzugefügt wird, während die westliche Art einem Bildhauer ähnelt, der aus dem Ganzen eines Steinblocks allmählich die Teile herausschält. Damit wird auch das Chaos der japanischen Metropolen und die völlige Abwesenheit einer übergeordneten Planfigur verständlich, was für Europäer so grauenerregend erscheint. Es ist die Dominanz der Teile über das Ganze. Das einzelne Haus ordnet sich nicht wie in abendländischen Städten dem Gesamtentwurf unter, sondern bleibt in einer aberwitzigen additiven Selbständigkeit bestehen.

Der Designer Masato Isaka vom Designbüro GK in Tokio nennt als sein Arbeitskonzept Mies van der Rohes berühmten Ausspruch »less is more«, der aber in Japan zu »more with less« gesteigert werde. Den Unterschied zu anderen Ländern beschreibt der Designer Tetsuyuki Hirano: »Japaner kümmern sich um jedes Detail und beachten bei jedem Produkt auch die kleinen Aspekte, während Entwerfer in Deutschland immer vom Gesamtkonzept ausgehen und das Produkt nur als logische Erweiterung der Funktion sehen.«[14]

Das Zusammenfügen von Details, die modulare »Bricolage«, die Kombination von heterogenen Elementen, ist typisch für den spielerischen Zugang zum Design. Das zeigt sich auch darin, daß nie verschiedene Materialien gemischt, sondern stets klar voneinander abgesetzt werden. Selbst die futuristisch-organischen Gestaltungen neuer Audio- und Videogeräte aus den Designabteilungen von Pioneer oder Yamaha, die wie eine abstrakte Synthese aus amerikanischem Streamline-Look und italienischem »Bolidismo« wirken, strahlen diese Selbstgenügsamkeit und Unabhängigkeit von Elementarformen aus und bleiben frei von jeglicher Monotonie und Gleichgültigkeit der deutschen Designklassiker.

In der Selbständigkeit der Teile, die erst durch Addition ein Ganzes ergeben, sieht der japanische Ökonom Fichi Sakiya auch die Grundstruktur des japanischen Gesellschaftslebens gespiegelt. In seinem Buch »Die Wissen-Wert-Revolution« von 1985 vergleicht er westliches Wissen mit einem Jumbo-Jet, dessen Einzelteile nicht perfekt sein müssen, aber so zusammenwirken, daß die Maschine fliegen kann. Japaner da-

which so appal Europeans. The whole is subordinate to the parts. The individual house is not (as in occidental cities) subordinate to an overall design; rather, it exists in an absurd, additive autonomy of its own.

The designer Masato Isaka, of GK Design Bureau in Tokyo, quotes as his working motto the architect Mies van der Rohe's famous dictum, »less is more« – though in Japan this is turned a notch or two higher, to »more with less«. The difference from other countries is described by the designer Tetsuyuki Hirano thus: »The Japanese pay attention to every detail, and with every product they take even minor aspects into account, whereas in Germany designers proceed from the overall concept and see the product purely as a logical extension of its function«.[14]

The Japanese conjoining of details, modular bricolage, the combination of heterogeneous elements, is characteristic of a ludic approach to design. We can see this, among other things, in the fact that different materials are never mixed, but always clearly distinguished and set apart. Even the futuristic/organic audio and video equipment designs by Pioneer and Yamaha, which look like an abstract synthesis of the American streamline look and Italian bolidismo, have this quality of a self-sufficiency and autonomy of basic form. They are altogether without the monotony and lustrelessness of German design classics.

The Japanese economist Fichi Sakiya sees in the autonomy of parts - that only become a whole through addition - a reflection of the fundamental structure of Japanese social life. In his 1985 book »The Knowledge-Value Revolution« he compares Western knowledge with a jumbo jet the individual parts of which do not need to be perfect as long as they work together in such a way that the craft will fly. The Japanese, on the other hand, are like a thousand clocks – all perfect down to the very last detail, yet not adding up to any more than the sum of their parts, a thousand clocks.[15]

The ever-increasing diversity of the products made by Japanese consumer electronics is deceptive; we might not notice that in fact the technical fundamentals of the equipment are increasingly similar. At first, manufacturers were constantly devising new combinations of functions. There were radios with recorder facilities,

n'est pas, comme en Occident, subordonnée à un plan d'ensemble, elle manifeste au contraire une autonomie rajoutée, incongrue.

Le designer Masato Isaka, du bureau GK Design à Tokyo, a fait sienne la célèbre devise de Mies van der Rohe «less is more» (le moins est le plus), ce qui est devenu au Japon «more with less» (le plus avec le moins). Le designer Tetsuyuki Hirano définit ainsi ce qui distingue le Japon des autres pays: «Les Japonais se soucient de chaque détail et considèrent aussi les aspects secondaires d'un produit, alors que les stylistes industriels allemands partent toujours du principe global et ne considèrent le produit que comme un développement logique de sa fonction».[14]

Le rassemblement de détails, le «bricolage» modulaire, la combinaison d'éléments hétérogènes, caractérise ces rapports ludiques avec le design. Cela se manifeste aussi par le fait que des matériaux différents ne sont jamais mélangés, mais se démarquent toujours nettement l'un de l'autre. Même les appareils sortis des bureaux de design de Pioneer ou Yamaha, dont l'aspect organo-futuriste fait l'effet d'une synthèse abstraite du Streamline-look américain et du «bolidismo» italien, semblent se suffire à eux-mêmes et être indépendants des formes élémentaires, et ils ne dégagent pas pas cette monotonie et cette indifférence qu'on observe chez les classiques du design allemand.

Cette autonomie des parties, qui ne produiront un Tout qu'en s'additionnant, reflète selon l'économiste japonais Fichi Sakiya, la structure élémentaire de la vie sociale japonaise. Dans son livre «La révolution de la valeur du savoir» paru en 1985, il compare le savoir occidental à un jumbo-jet, dont les éléments sans être parfaits doivent coopérer de telle sorte que la machine puisse voler. Les Japonais, par contre, sont comme mille montres, chacune parfaite en soi, mais dont le Tout ne sera jamais plus que la somme des parties, c'est-à-dire mille montres.[15]

Cette variété toujours plus grande des «consumer electronics» japonais nous cache le fait que les modules de construction de ces appareils se ressemblent de plus en plus. Au début les fabricants innovaient sans cesse des combinaisons de fonctions. Il y avait des radiomagnétophones, des magnétophones avec TV, des montres-radios,

gegen seien wie tausend Uhren, alle perfekt bis ins Detail, die aber in der Summe doch nicht mehr als tausend Uhren ergeben.[15]

Die immer größere Produktvielfalt japanischer »consumer electronics« täuscht darüber hinweg, daß sich die technischen Bausteine der Geräte immer ähnlicher werden. Anfangs erfanden die Hersteller ständig neue Kombinationen von Funktionen. Es gab Radios mit Recorder, Recorder mit TV's, Uhren mit Radios, Recorder mit Uhren und wahre Multifunktions-Cockpits mit allen denkbaren Audio-Video-Geräten, die als Rackets und Hifi-Türme die Wohnzimmer eroberten. Heute geht die Bausteinlogik bis in die Mikroelektronik, in der die gleichen Komponenten immer neue Konfigurationen bilden. Es ergießt sich eine endlose Flut von Schaltkreisen, Halbleitern, Mikrochips, Flüssigkristalldisplays und LED-Anzeigen in die Fertigungshallen, wo die Hersteller sie zu immer neuen Konstellationen verbinden. Diese Kreuzungs- und Zwitterprodukte können abwechselnd Kameras, Recorder, Disc-Player, Taschenrechner, Autotelefone oder Fernbedienungen werden. Es sind Geräte für verschiedene Zwecke, die aber immer mehr aus den gleichen Mitteln bestehen.

Diese uhrwerkhafte Präzision ist auch die Basis der Leistungsfähigkeit der japanischen Industrie. Seit der Erfindung der »lean production«, der »schlanken Fertigung«, gibt es kaum mehr zentralisierte Massenfertigungsunternehmen. Die Herstellung von immer mehr Bausteinen wird ausgelagert und an Zulieferer übertragen, die oft sogar die Forschung und Entwicklung übernehmen. Dieses knallharte »outsourcing«, die Ausgliederung von Produktionsstufen, hat die Fertigungstiefe japanischer Hersteller drastisch vermindert. Zehntausende semi-autonomer kleiner Firmen stehen in hartem Konkurrenzkampf um die Belieferung der Großkonzerne, die ihre Aufwendungen und Investitionen nahezu halbieren konnten. Dasselbe gilt für die Fabrikarbeiter, die weitaus höher qualifiziert sind als etwa in Amerika. Sie konzentrieren sich nicht nur auf monofunktionale Arbeitsstufen, sondern erfüllen am Fließband Mehrzweckfunktionen wie Reparaturen, Qualitätskontrollen, das Richten von Teilen und Werkzeugen, für die im Westen Heere spezialisierter Fabriktechniker zuständig sind.[16]

tape recorders with TVs, clocks with radios, tape decks with clocks, and whole multifunctional cockpits of every conceivable kind of audio and video gadget, invading our living rooms in their hifi racks. Now, the principle of interchangeable components has extended even into micro-electronics, where the same parts are forever being arranged ·in new configurations. Hence the endless flood of circuitries, semiconductors, microchips, liquid crystal displays and LED read-outs on production lines – where the manufacturers are forever combining them anew. These crossbred or dual-character products may turn out to be cameras, tape decks, CD players, pocket calculators, car phones or remote controls. The purposes of the products may vary, but increasingly they are being made of the selfsame components.

This clockwork precision is also the foundation of Japanese industry's sheer performance. Ever since lean production was thought up, centralized mass-production firms have been increasingly thin on the ground. More and more components are being subcontracted out to supply manufacturers who often even answer for research and product development. This blatant outsourcing has drastically cut the production depth of Japanese manufacturers. Tens of thousands of semi-autonomous firms are now competing fiercely to supply the major companies, which have been able almost to halve their expenses and investments. The same applies to factory workers, who are far better qualified than in (say) America. They not only concentrate on single-function work stages, but apply a variety of skills on the assembly line: repairs, quality control, or preparing parts and tools – all tasks that require armies of specialist factory technicians in the West.[16]

Outsourcing and sectional relocation entered the design departments some years ago. The companies established satellite studios to liberate designers from production pressures. It is no accident that these offices tend to be in Tokyo's entertainment districts, where contact with consumer society is at its most immediate and intimate. Thus Matsushita's design studio operates in Roppongi, Hitachi's in Ayoyama, and Seiko's in Minami-Aoyama. What is relatively recent is subcontracting to freelance designers. In Japan to date they have less

des montres avec système d'enregistrement et de véritables cockpits polyvalents avec tous les appareils audio-vidéo imaginables qui envahirent les salons. Aujourd'hui, on a atteint le stade de la microélectronique dans laquelle les mêmes composants créeront toujours de nouvelles configurations. Les usines produisent un flot de circuits de commutation, de semiconducteurs, de microchips, d'affichages à cristaux liquides, d'annonces électroluminescentes aux combinaisons sans cesse nouvelles. Ces produits hybrides peuvent devenir des caméras, des lecteurs de cassettes, des platines, des calculatrices, des téléphones mobiles ou des télécommandes. Ce sont des appareils conçus pour des objectifs différents, mais qui sont de plus en plus composés des mêmes pièces.

Cette précision d'horloge est aussi la base des performances de l'industrie japonaise. Depuis qu'on a inventé la «lean production», la fabrication légère, les centres de fabrication en série se font rares. Des entreprises de sous-traitance produisent de plus en plus de modules, et se chargent également souvent de la recherche et du développement. Ce «out sourcing» radical, la séparation des stades de fabrication, a réduit de manière saisissante la concentration verticale des entreprises japonaises. Dix mille petites entreprises semi-autonomes s'efforcent d'être le plus compétitives possible pour livrer les grands konzerns dont les charges et les investissements ont presque diminué de moitié.

Le même principe est valable pour les ouvriers d'usine dont les qualifications sont bien supérieures à celles de leurs homologues américains. Ils ne se concentrent pas seulement sur des étapes de travail spécifiques, mais remplissent des tâches diverses sur la chaîne de fabrication – comme réparations, contrôles de qualité, ajustage de pièces et d'outils. En Occident, en emploie à cet effet des légions de techniciens spécialisés [16].

Le «out sourcing» apparut aussi il y a quelques années dans les services de design. Les groupes industriels créèrent des studios satellites pour libérer les concepteurs de la pression due à la production. Ce n'est pas un hasard si ces bureaux se trouvent le plus souvent dans les secteurs de Tokyo où l'on s'amuse, là où le contact avec la société de consommation est le plus intense. C'est ainsi que l'atelier de Matsushita travaille à

Das »outsourcing« und die Auslagerung begannen vor einigen Jahren auch mit den Design-Abteilungen. Die Konzerne gründeten Satellitenstudios, um die Entwerfer vom Produktionsdruck zu befreien. Diese Büros sind nicht zufällig meistens in den Vergnügungsbezirken von Tokio angesiedelt, wo die Tuchfühlung mit der »consumer society« am größten ist. So arbeitet das Design-Atelier von Matsushita in Roppongi, das von Hitachi in Ayoyama und Seiko in Minami-Aoyama. Relativ neu ist die Auftragsvergabe an freie Designer. Sie haben bislang in Japan noch weniger eine selbständige Tradition als die Architekten, von denen mittlerweile immerhin zwanzig Prozent außerhalb der riesigen Baukonzerne eigene Büros unterhalten.

Die neue japanische Design-Offensive setzt gerade erst ein. Bei allen eigenen Begabungen waren japanische Gestalter jahrzehntelang einzig an westlichen Entwicklungen orientiert und reisten als Gastarbeiter durch alle großen Studios der Welt, um die neusten Erfindungen heimzuholen. Masaki Morita beispielsweise brachte prägende Eindrücke von seinem einjährigen Finnlandaufenthalt mit, Masanori Umeda arbeitete mehrere Jahre für Memphis in Mailand, und der 1991 verstorbene Altmeister Shiro Kuramata antizipierte die bunte italienische Postmoderne wie auch den nachfolgenden Dekonstruktivismus um Jahre. Die bislang nur geringe Innovationsgabe der Japaner im Design weicht heute einem Ausbruch vormals unterdrückter Kreativität, die sich endlich der westlichen Ketten entwunden hat. Masaki Morita spricht sogar von einer »Re-Japonisierung« der japanischen Gestaltung, um die kulturellen Eigenheiten wiederzuentdecken. Es kursiert unter Gestaltern das Wort von der »Donut-Kultur«, das die ausgehöhlte japanische Identität mit jenen amerikanischen Zuckerkuchen vergleicht, in deren Mitte ein Loch gähnt.

Die in diesem Buch ausgewählten Beispiele neuer japanischer Gestaltung wollen keinen repräsentativen, sondern einen signifikanten Querschnitt bieten. Es geht darum, neuen Ansätzen einer Individualisierung der japanischen Ästhetik nachzuforschen, auch wenn die vorgestellten Beispiele oft noch nicht über das Stadium von Prototypen hinausgelangt sind. Weil der Wirtschaftserfolg die Japaner völlig von sich selbst entfremdet hat, steckt selbst in den verrücktesten neuen Artefakten der

of an independent tradition than architects, a respectable 20 per cent of whom now work from their own offices outside the huge construction firms.

The new Japanese design offensive is only beginning. Talented in their own right though they were, Japanese designers took their bearings for decades purely from Western developments. They travelled the world, working for spells in the studios of others, and returned home with the latest inventions in their luggage. For example, Masaki Morita returned from a one-year stay in Finland with vital impressions; Masanori Umeda worked for Memphis in Milan for several years; and the revered Shiro Kuramata, who died in 1991, anticipated by years colourful Italian post-modernism and the deconstructionism that followed. The Japanese talent for design innovation was hitherto a modest one, but now we are seeing an outburst of suppressed creativity that is finally breaking loose of the West. Masaki Morita even speaks of a »re-Japanization« of Japanese design, a rediscovery of qualities specific to Japanese culture. Designers elsewhere speak of a »donut culture«, comparing the hollow Japanese identity with the American-style doughnut with a hole in the centre.

The examples of contemporary Japanese design selected for this book do not aim to cover the ground representatively. Rather, they afford a cross-section. They document the tendency towards a new individualization of Japanese aesthetics. Economic success has alienated the Japanese from themselves, and one result is that even in the most outlandish of new artefacts we can detect a wish to step back from Western models. Charles Jencks sees the great advantage of the Japanese in the fact that they do not regard the reconciliation of opposites as any kind of contradiction in terms: »Japanese everyday life is made up of opposites: Western dress and kimonos, a Western view of democracy and traditional social structures.«[17] When Kuramata adorns his subtle, minimalist perspex wall screens and furniture with flower inlays as tenderly evocative of Nature as any haiku, when Shigeru Uchida introduces drama

Roppongi, celui de Hitachi à Ayoyama et celui de Seiko à Minami-Aoyama. Depuis relativement peu de temps, on passe des commandes à des designers indépendants. Jusqu'ici, ils étaient traditionnellement encore moins autonomes que les architectes, dont malgré tout 20 pour cent ont entre temps leurs propres bureaux à côté des géants industriels.

On assiste à une nouvelle offensive du design japonais. Bien que très doués, les créateurs japonais se sont orientés pendant des décennies uniquement sur les évolutions occidentales, et ils ont voyagé et ont travaillé dans les studios du monde entier pour ramener chez eux les inventions les plus récentes. Masaki Morita, par exemple, ramena des impressions marquantes de son séjour en Finlande, Masanori Umeda travailla plusieurs années pour Memphis à Milan, et Shiro Kuramata, leur aîné, mort en 1991, anticipa avec des années d'avance le mouvement post-moderne italien aux couleurs vives, aussi bien que le déconstructivisme qui suivit. Le manque de créativité constaté chez les stylistes japonais est de l'histoire ancienne. On assiste à une explosion de cette créativité longtemps réprimée, et qui a réussi à se dégager des entraves occidentales. Masaki Morita évoque même une «rejaponisation» qui va redécouvrir les particularités culturelles. On parle aussi d'une «culture des donuts», pour comparer l'identité japonaise vidée de sa substance à la pâtisserie américaine trouée en son milieu.

Les exemples du nouveau design japonais sélectionnés dans ce livre ne veulent pas proposer un profil représentatif, mais un profil signifiant. Il s'agit d'analyser les nouveaux départs d'une individualisation de l'esthétique japonaise. Le succès économique a complètement aliéné les Japonais, et c'est pourquoi, même dans les nouvelles créations les plus folles, il existe le désir de se détacher complètement des modèles occidentaux. Pour Charles Jencks, les Japonais ont un avantage colossal, car à leurs yeux les contraires ne sont pas incompatibles: «La vie quotidienne au Japon est remplie de contradictions: vêtements occidentaux et kimonos, compréhension toute occidentale de la démocratie et statuts sociaux traditionnels.»[17] Que Kuramata conçoive des murs et des meubles de plexiglas subtilement minimalistes avec des insertions délicates de fleurs faisant songer à la puissance

Wunsch, sich den abendländischen Vorbildern zu entziehen. Den gewaltigen Vorteil der Japaner sieht Charles Jencks darin, daß sie keinen Widerspruch darin finden, Gegensätze zu vereinen: »Der japanische Alltag ist ein Leben mit Gegensätzen: westliche Kleidung und Kimono, westliches Demokratieverständnis und traditionelle Gesellschaftsordnung.«[17] Ob Kuramata minimalistisch-subtile Plexiglaswände und -möbel mit zarten Blumen-Inlays wie Haiku-Naturandeutungen entwirft, Shigeru Uchida seine Räume mit tempelartigen Stahlwänden und Säulenreihen dramatisiert oder Masanori Umeda das grobschlächtige Spielzeugdesign von Memphis mit japanischer Feingliedrigkeit weiterentwickelt – immer geht es zugleich um die Rückeroberung einer verlorenen Tradition als auch um die Entdeckung von Neuland, für das es noch keine ästhetische Landkarte gibt.

Aber nicht nur den westlichen Überfremdungen, sondern auch dem Konsumismus allgemein sagen immer mehr Designer den Kampf an. Seitdem in Japan sogar das MITI die Firmen auffordert, den extrem schnellen Modellwechsel zu stoppen und mehr auf langlebige Produkte hinzuarbeiten, ist der Überdruß am oberflächlichen Massendesign offenbar geworden. Die Strategien der Japaner zur Individualisierung der Produkte und Designs zielen deutlich auf eine Verlangsamung der Verschleißgeschwindigkeit. Objekte werden gleichsam mit ästhetischen Widerhaken gespickt, die Funktionen müssen sich den Formen anpassen. Selbst das neue Retro-Design von Nissan-Autos wie »Pao« oder »Figaro« oder von Sharp-Radios im Look der fünfziger Jahre läßt sich als Teil dieser ästhetischen Differenzierung verstehen. Denn jahrzehntelang waren die Japaner gleichsam die »Streber« auf dem Weltmarkt, die immer nur nach vorn schauten und jetzt mit nostalgischen Entwürfen einen Hang zum Konservativismus verraten.

Dieser Retro-Look stellt eine der interessantesten neuen Entwicklungen in der japanischen Gestaltung dar, die Auswege aus dem Dilemma des gesichtslosen Massendesigns sucht. Im Westen gibt es seit einigen Jahren ein ähnliches Phänomen, das den ewig neuen Hervorbringungen der Konsumwelt mit künstlichen Gebrauchsspuren begegnet. Es ist das, was Alessandro Mendini einmal als »Instantiquariat« be-

into spaces by using temple-like steel walls and rows of columns, or when Masanori Umeda takes the crude toy-like design of Memphis a step further with Japanese sensitivity, the core concern is always to recover a lost tradition as much as to discover new territory for which there is as yet no aesthetic map.

More and more designers are attempting to combat not only alien Western input but indeed consumerism in general. Even MITI has been calling on companies to halt the over-rapid changeover of models and to work for products with a longer life; and, in the wake of that requirement, a sated weariness with shallow mass design has become more and more apparent. Japanese strategies to individualize products and designs are quite plainly aimed at slowing down the pace of wear and tear. New creations are having the brakes built into them, so to speak. Functions are now having to adapt to form. Even the new retrodesign of Nissan cars such as the Pao or Figaro, or Sharp radios in Fifties style, could be seen as part of this aesthetic differentiation. For decades, after all, the Japanese were the ones who wanted to get ahead in the global market place; and now their nostalgic designs are signalling a leaning towards conservatism.

The retrolook is one of the most interesting new developments in Japanese design, which is seeking ways out of the faceless anonymity of mass design. For some years we have been witnessing a similar phenomenon in the West. The perpetual newness of the consumer world has been countered by artificial signs of use. Alessandro Mendini once called it »instant ageing«, and it is best seen in the stonewashed look of certain jeans, which come brand new from the factory and yet have an aged, worn look. Historicizing product design aims similarly to increase value by grafting on a patina of traditional ornamentation. The products in question may often only be what are known as pike products – such as the Nissan Figaro – which can only be produced in small, collectors' runs owing to the costly production method. But these products are conferring on manufacturers known for the facelessness of their design a newly design-conscious image. And they are courting symbolic values not very far below the threshold that the independent designers

d'évocation des Haiku, que Shigeru Uchida dramatise ses espaces à l'aide de murs d'acier et de rangées de colonnes dignes d'un temple, ou que Masanori Umeda développe le design grossier du jouet de Memphis en l'agrémentant de détails d'une finesse toute japonaise, il s'agit toujours aussi bien de reconquérir une tradition perdue que de découvrir une terre inconnue dont la carte esthétique n'est pas encore tracée.

Mais les stylistes sont de plus en plus nombreux à déclarer la guerre non seulement aux apports occidentaux mais aussi à la consommation en général. Depuis qu'au Japon même MITI demande aux entreprises de mettre une fin à la valse endiablée des modèles et de développer plutôt des produits plus durables, il est manifeste que les gens en ont assez du design de série artificiel. Les stratégies développées par les Japonais pour individualiser davantage les produits et les designs vont nettement dans le sens d'un ralentissement de la vitesse d'usure. Les objets sont pour ainsi dire lardés de crochets esthétiques, les fonctions doivent s'adapter aux formes. On peut même percevoir cette différenciation esthétique dans le nouveau style rétro des automobiles Nissan, comme «Pao» ou «Figaro», ou des radios Sharp aux allures des années 50. Pendant des décennies, les Japonais ont été les arrivistes sur le marché mondial, ceux qui regardaient toujours en avant, et ils trahissent maintenant avec leurs créations un penchant pour le conservatisme.

Ce style rétro, une tentative pour échapper au marasme de la fabrication en série anonyme, représente pour le design japonais une des évolutions les plus intéressantes de ces dernières années. En Occident, on observe depuis quelques années un phénomène semblable, et les nouveautés qui sortent sans arrêt sont parées de traces d'utilisation artificielles. Alessandro Mendini appelait cela l'«instantiquariat» dont les «stone-washed jeans», qui sortent déjà usés de l'usine, sont le meilleur exemple. La présentation ancienne du produit par la patine artificielle est également conçue pour le mettre en valeur. Il ne s'agit souvent que de ce que l'on appelle les «pike-products» ou produits piques, le Nissan Figaro, par exemple, qui ne sort qu'en nombre limité comme pièce de collection à cause de sa fabrication compliquée. Mais ils permettent

zeichnete und was sich am deutlichsten im »stone-washed look« der Jeansmode zeigte, die fabrikneu und dennoch gealtert ist. Auch die historisierende Produktgestaltung zielt auf ähnliche Wertsteigerung durch die scheinbare Patina tradierter Schmuckformen. Dabei handelt es sich oft nur um sogenannte Pike-Products oder Speerspitzenprodukte, etwa der Nissan Figaro, die wegen der aufwendigen Herstellung nur in kleinen Auflagen als Sammlerobjekte herauskommen. Aber sie verhelfen bislang gesichtslosen Massenherstellern zu einem designbewußten Image und kultivieren Symbolwerte knapp unterhalb der Schwelle, die die in diesem Buch vorgestellten freien Designer endgültig übertreten haben.

Dabei haben die Japaner einen Generalvorteil: Gegenüber der rücksichtslosen Naturbeherrschung im Abendland hat die japanische Kultur einen viel engeren und sensibleren Bezug zu Naturelementen; Formbildungen orientieren sich stets am Maßstab des menschlichen Körpers und seinen Vitalfunktionen. Wenn die Japaner ihre Design-Tugenden ähnlich erfindungsreich und leistungsfähig entwickeln wie zuvor ihre Fähigkeit zur Produktion hochwertiger Massengüter, dann dürften die nächsten Jahre ganz im Zeichen der aufgehenden Sonne stehen.

featured in this book have crossed. The Japanese have one general advantage. In the West, Nature is under humankind's ruthless thumb, whereas Japanese civilization has a far closer, more sensitive sense of Nature. Formal characteristics are defined in relation to the human body's proportions and vital functions. If the Japanese evolve their design virtues with as great a capacity for inventiveness and performance as they did their ability to produce quality mass market goods, the years ahead will be dominated by the Rising Sun.

à des fabricants de série jusqu'ici anonymes de retrouver une image au niveau de leur design, et ils cultivent des valeurs symboliques juste en deçà du seuil que les designers présentés dans cet ouvrage ont définitivement franchi.

Les Japonais ont à cet égard un avantage d'ordre général: alors que les Occidentaux dominent la Nature sans aucun ménagement, les Japonais ont des relations beaucoup plus étroites et sensibles avec les éléments naturels; les formes s'orientent toujours sur les critères du corps humain et ses fonctions vitales. Et si les Japonais deviennent aussi inventifs et performants au niveau du design qu'ils l'ont été auparavant au niveau de la fabrication de produits de série de grande qualité, les années à venir devraient être placées sous le signe du Soleil Levant.

ANMERKUNGEN

1 »Die Nachfrage sinkt bereits, wenn ein Produkt gerade erst ein Hit geworden ist«. Aussage von Kiyoshi Sakashita, Direktor des Sharp-Design-center, zit. nach »The Power of Design«, in: Business Tokio, Dezember 1991
2 Kazuo Shinohara, »Chaos and Machine«, The Japan Architect, Nr. 5, 1988.
3 Roland Barthes, Das Reich der Zeichen, Suhrkamp-Verlag, Frankfurt am Main 1981
4 Vergleiche die glänzende Untersuchung von Klaus Berger, »Japonismus in der westlichen Malerei 1860-1920«, Prestel-Verlag, München 1980. Dort wird der nicht-humanistische Naturalismus der ja-panischen Farbholzschnitte und ihre auf naturreli-giösem Pantheismus beruhende Lebensauffassung beschrieben und in ihrem Einfluß auf die französi-schen Malerfürsten erforscht.
5 Walter Gropius im Vorwort eines Fotobandes über den Katsura Palast, Yale University, 1960, zit. nach Reyner Banham / Hiroyuki Suzuki, Modernes Bauen in Japan. Deutsche Verlagsanstalt, Stuttgart 1987, S. 17
6 Kenji Ekuan, »Design als Überlebensprinzip«, in: Design Report Nr. 14, Frankfurt 1990, S. 59.
7 »What makes Yoshio invent« in: The Economist v. 18. Januar 1991.
8 »How Sony innovates«, in: Fortune v. 24. Februar 1992.
9 Hugh Aldersey-Williams, Nationalism and Globalism in Design. Rizzoli, New York 1992, S. 144-154.
10 Hans Wichmann, »Industrial Design - Die neue Sammlung«. Prestel-Verlag, München 1985. S. 410
11 Penny Sparke, Japanisches Design. Westermann-Verlag, Braunschweig 1988, S. 15.
12 Yoshinobu Ashihara, The Hidden Order. Kodansha International, Tokio und New York 1989, S. 21.
13 ebenda, S. 68.
14 Hugh Aldersey-Williams, a.a.O., S. 148
15 Zit. nach Frankfurter Allgemeine Zeitung, v. 29. Februar 1992, Wochenendbeilage, S.2
16 »Das wird die Welt verändern«, Reportage über japanische Industriearbeit, in: Der Spiegel v. 8. April 1991
17 Charles Jencks, »The Pluralism of Recent Japanese Architecture«, RSA-Journal, November 1979, S. 748

NOTES

1 »The demand already starts to fall when a product has just become a hit.« Thus Kiyoshi Sakashita, director of the Sharp Design Centre, in »The Power of Design«, Business Tokyo, December 1991.
2 Kazuo Shinohara, »Chaos and Machine«, The Japan Architect 5, 1988.
3 Roland Barthes, L'Empire des Signes, Editions d'Art Albert Skira, Genève 1970
4 Cf. Klaus Berger's excellent study, »Japonismus in der westlichen Malerei 1860-1920«, Prestel, Munich 1980. Berger analyzes the non-humanist naturalism of Japanese coloured woodcuts and their pantheistic view of life, and examines their influence on eminent French artists.
5 Walter Gropius, in the foreword to a book of photographs of Katsura Palace (Yale University Press, 1960), quoted from Reyner Banham and Hiroyuki Suzuki: Modernes Bauen in Japan, Deutsche Verlagsanstalt, Stuttgart 1987, p. 17.
6 Kenji Ekuan, »Design als Überlebensprinzip«, Design Report 14, Frankfurt 1990, p. 59.
7 »What makes Yoshio invent«, The Economist, 18 January 1991.
8 »How Sony innovates«, Fortune, 24 February 1992.
9 Hugh Aldersey-Williams, Nationalism and Globalism in Design, Rizzoli, New York 1992, pp. 144-154.
10 Hans Wichmann, »Industrial Design - Die neue Sammlung«, Prestel, Munich 1985, p. 410.
11 Penny Sparke, Japanisches Design, Westermann, Braunschweig 1988, p. 15.
12 Yoshinobu Ashihara, The Hidden Order, Kodansha International, Tokyo and New York 1989, p. 21.
13 ibid, p, 68.
14 Aldersey-Williams, op. cit., p. 148.
15 Frankfurter Allgemeine Zeitung weekend supple-ment, 29 February 1992, p.2.
16 »Das wird die Welt verändern«, Der Spiegel, 8 April 1991.
17 Charles Jencks, »The Pluralism of Recent Japanese Architecture«, RSA Journal, November 1979, p. 748.

REMARQUES

1 «La demande baisse déjà quand un produit vient de devenir un tube». Citation de Kiyoshi Sakashita, directeur du centre de Design Sharp, extraite de «The Power of Design», in Business, Tokyo, décembre 1991.
2 Kazuo Shinohara, «Chaos and Machine», The Japan Architect, n°5, 1988.
3 Roland Barthes, L'Empire des Signes, Editions d'Art Albert Skira, Genève 1970
4 A comparer avec l'enquête brillante de Klaus Berger, «Japonismus in der westlichen Malerei 1860-1920». Prestel-Verlag, Munich 1980. L'ouvrage décrit le naturalisme non humaniste des estampes japonaises et leur conception de la vie qui repose sur un panthéisme divinisant la Nature, et analyse son influence sur les maîtres de la pein-ture française.
5 Walter Gropius dans la préface à son album sur le Palais Katsura, Yale University, 1960, cité d'après Reyner Banham/Hiroyuki Suzuki, Modernes Bauen in Japan, Deutsche Verlagsanstalt, Stuttgart 1987, p. 17.
6 Kenji Ekuan, «Design als Überlebensprinzip», in: Design Report n° 14, Francfort 1990, p. 59.
7 «What makes Yoshio invent» in: The Economist du 18 janvier 1991.
8 «How Sony innovates», in: Fortune du 24 février 1992.
9 Hugh Aldersey-Williams, Nationalism and Globalism in Design. Rizzoli, New York 1992, pp. 144-154.
10 Hans Wichmann, «Industrial Design - Die neue Sammlung», Prestel-Verlag, Munich 1985, p. 410.
11 Penny Sparke, Japanisches Design. Westermann-Verlag, Brunswick 1988, p. 15.
12 Yoshinobu Ashihara, The Hidden Order, Kodansha International, Tokyo et New York 1989, p. 21.
13 ibid., p. 68.
14 H. Aldersey-Williams, ouvrage cité ci-dessus, p.148
15 Cité d'après le Frankfurter Allgemeine Zeitung du 29 février 1992, supplément du week-end, p. 2.
16 «Das wird die Welt verändern», reportage sur le travail industriel japonais in: Der Spiegel du 8 avril 1991.
17 Charles Jencks, «The Pluralism of Recent Japanese Architecture», RSA-Journal, novembre 1979, p. 748.

Memphis Ginza, 1982
Regal, shelf, étagère

Design Masanori Umeda

MASAKI MORITA

MASAKI MORITA

1950	Geboren in der Präfektur Kumamoto
1974	Aufenthalt in Finnland und Heirat mit seiner finnischen Frau Marjatta
1975	Diplom an der Kuwasawa Design Schule in Tokio
1976	Gründung des Studios »Design M«
1980	Preis der Japan Commercial Design Association

1950	Born in Kumamoto Prefecture
1974	Lengthy stay in Finland. Marries a Finnish woman, Marjatta
1975	Diploma from Kuwasawa Design School, Tokyo
1976	Establishes »Design M« Studio
1980	Japanese Commercial Design Association prize

1950	Naît dans la circonscription de Kumamoto
1974	Séjour en Finlande et mariage avec une Finnoise, Marjatta
1975	Diplôme de l'Ecole de Design de Kuwasawa à Tokyo
1976	Création du studio «Design M»
1980	Prix du Japan Commercial Design Association

Das größte Leitbild für Masaki Morita war lange Zeit Shiro Kuramata und dessen Minimalismus. Doch die Omnipräsenz Kuramatas ließ jüngeren Entwerfern kaum Spielraum, weshalb Morita sich von dem Altmeister abkehrte. Seine Entwürfe sind konzeptionell, ohne minimalistisch zu sein. Gegen den monofunktionalen Symbolismus europäischer Gebrauchsdinge setzt er mehrdeutige Entwürfe. Seinen Stil könnte man als »Neo-Komfortabilismus« bezeichnen. Morita kreiert Luxusobjekte für die Gefühle. Sie wollen mehr bieten als bloße Funktionalität. Seine Vorliebe für elementare Materialien wie Stein, Stahl und Glas und seine zuweilen zoomorphen Formen sind bei aller Abstraktion stark von Naturbezügen geprägt. Grelle Farben empfindet er als künstlich und benutzt am liebsten dunkle Töne. Als bösen Kommentar zum japanischen Anti-Individualismus und Gruppenzwang entwarf er eine Serie Robotermöbel, um die japanischen Maschinenmenschen zu karikieren.

For a long time, Masaki Morita's great model was Shiro Kuramata and his minimalism. But the omnipresence of Kuramata scarcely left younger designers any room to manoeuvre, and so Morita turned away from the old master. His designs are conceptual without being minimalist; in contrast to the monofunctional symbolism of European utility objects, they are multivalent. His style might be termed neo-Comfortablism. Morita's creations are luxury objects for the feelings, aiming to offer more than mere functionality. His preference for basic materials such as stone, steel and glass, together with his occasionally zoomorphic shapes, show a strong sense of Nature, for all his abstraction. He sees bright colours as artificial, and prefers dark shades. By way of a wicked commentary on Japanese anti-individualism and compulsively collective behaviour he designed a series of robot furniture as a spoof on Japanese automaton people.

Le grand modèle de Masaki Morita a longtemps été Shiro Kuramata, le maître de l'art minimal. Mais l'omniprésence de Kuramata laissait très peu de place aux jeunes créateurs, et Morita se détacha de lui pour cette raison. Ses projections sont conceptionnelles sans être minimalistes. Il répond au symbolisme monovalent des pièces utilitaires européennes par des créations polysémiques. Son style pourrait se nommer la «néo-confortabilité». Morita crée des objets de luxe qui veulent nous émouvoir, offrir davantage que la pure fonctionnalité. Sa préférence pour les matériaux élémentaires comme la pierre, l'acier et le verre et ses formes parfois zoomorphiques sont, toute abstraction retenue, très marquées par des références naturalistes. Il trouve les couleurs vives artificielles, et utilise plus volontiers des tons sombres. Sa série de meubles-robots, caricatures des hommes-machines japonais, commente méchamment l'anti-individualisme et la pression sociale qui règnent au Japon.

Kintoun, 1988
Sofa, sofa, canapé

The Earth
Sitz-Objekt, seating design, siège

p. 31
Kintoun, 1988
Sofa, sofa, canapé

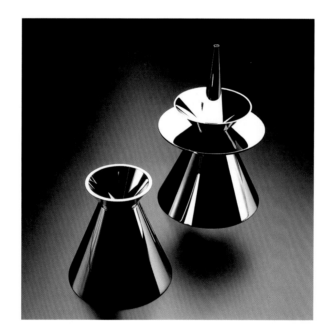

Himaraya, 1991
Aschenbecher, ashtray, cendrier

Mr. & Mrs. Ash, 1986
Aschenbecher, ashtray, cendrier

Non Brand Furniture
Stuhl, chair, chaise

Non Brand Furniture
Hocker, stool, tabouret

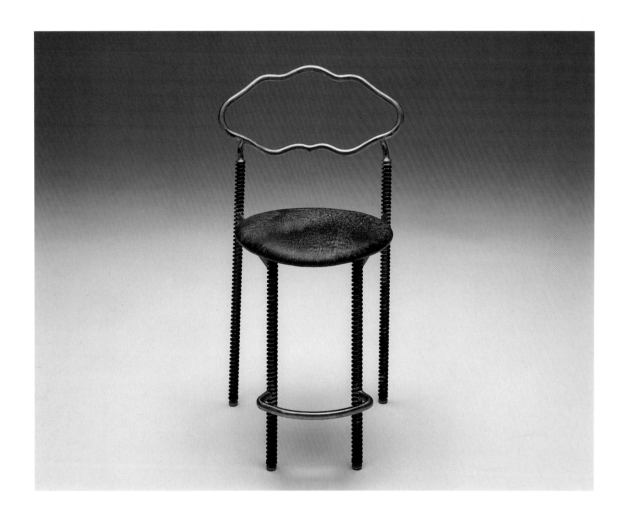

Amoeba, 1980
Stuhl, chair, chaise

Valentine, 1983
Stuhl, chair, chaise

Red Sofa, 1989
Sofa, sofa, canapé

p. 37
Blue Sofa, 1989
Sofa, sofa, canapé

AV Terior, 1989
Boutique
Minami-Ikebukuro, Tokyo

Dancing Table, 1990
Tisch, table, table

p. 41
Swing Lotus, 1990
Sessel, armchair, fauteuil

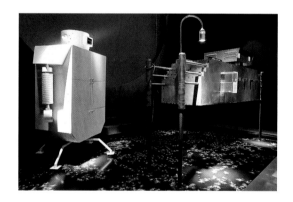

Shi Shi, 1982
Regal-Objekt, shelf-unit, étagère

Tsuchiya-Kun & Cani-San, 1982
Kommode, mit Video- und Audiocontainer (links)
Sideboard with audio/video compartment (left)
Commode avec conteneur audio-vidéo (à gauche)

p. 43
Tsuchiya-Kun, 1982
Schrank mit Digitaluhr, cabinet with digital clock,
armoire avec montre digitale

MASANORI UMEDA

MASANORI UMEDA

1941	Geboren in Kanagawa
1962	Diplom an der Kuwasawa Design Schule in Tokio
1967-69	Mitarbeit im Studio Castiglioni in Mailand
1970-79	Designberater für Olivetti
1981-83	Mitarbeiter bei Memphis
1986	Gründung des eigenen Studios U-Meta Design in Tokio

1941	Born in Kanagawa
1962	Diploma from Kuwasawa Design School, Tokyo
1967-69	Works at Studio Castiglioni, Milan
1970-79	Design consultant for Olivetti
1981-83	Works for Memphis
1986	Founds his own studio, U-Meta Design, in Tokyo

1941	Naît à Kanagawa
1962	Diplôme de l'Ecole de Design de Kuwasawa à Tokyo
1967-69	Collaborateur au Studio Castiglioni à Milan
1970-79	Conseiller en design pour Olivetti
1981-83	Collaborateur chez Memphis
1986	Création de l'atelier U-Meta Design à Tokyo

Durch seinen Wohlstand hat Japan die Schönheit seiner Natur zerstört, sagt der vielseitige Industrie-, Experimental- und Interieurdesigner Masanori Umeda. Trotz ihres ökonomischen Reichtums sind die Häuser und Wohnungen der Japaner oft von erbärmlicher Armut gekennzeichnet. Um die Wurzeln der japanischen Kultur, ihren intensiven Einklang mit Landschaft, Witterung und Pflanzenwelt wiederzuentdecken, greifen Umedas Möbel Motive von Pflaumenbäumen, Kirschblüten und Seerosen auf. Es sind Naturandeutungen, die die Ästhetik von Flower-Power und Pop-Art der sechziger Jahre weiterentwickeln. Bei seinen abstrakteren Möbel-, Geschirr- und Interieur-Entwürfen zeigt sich seine Prägung durch Memphis, die er aber mit japanischer Feingliedrigkeit weiterentwickelt. Seine bekannte Möbel-Ikone »Tawaraya«, das Boxring-Bett, ist als bissig-ironischer Kommentar zum neuen Freistil-Design wie auch zum Überlebenskampf im überbevölkerten Japan zu verstehen.

Through its affluence, Japan has destroyed its own natural beauty, claims the versatile industrial, experimental and interior designer Masanori Umeda. Despite their economic wealth, the Japanese live in houses and flats that are often wretchedly poor. Umeda's furniture uses motifs of plum trees, cherry blossoms and lotuses in order to rediscover the roots of Japanese culture and its intense harmony with the landscape, weather and plant kingdom. These plant references continue the 1960s aesthetics of flower power and pop art. In his abstract furniture, crockery and interior designs, Umeda reveals his Memphis influence, though he pursues the line with Japanese finesse. »Tawaraya«, a boxingring bed and his best-known piece of furniture, is a bitingly ironic commentary on new free-style design and equally on the struggle to survive in the new overcrowded Japan.

La prospérité du Japon est la cause de la disparition des beautés de sa Nature, dit Masanori Umeda, designer aux multiples talents qui travaille pour l'industrie, au niveau expérimental, et crée des intérieurs. Le Japon est un pays riche et pourtant, les maisons et logements de ses habitants sont souvent d'une pauvreté lamentable. Pour retrouver les racines de la culture japonaise, son harmonie intense avec le paysage, la flore et le temps qu'il fait, les meubles de Umeda s'inspirent des pruniers, des fleurs de cerisier et des nénuphars. Ce sont des allusions à la Nature qui font évoluer l'esthétisme du flower-power et du pop-art des années soixante. Ses créations plus abstraites de meubles, de vaisselle et d'intérieurs montrent l'influence de Memphis, tempérée par la finesse des formes japonaises. Son célèbre meuble iconique «Tawaraya», le lit boxring, est à interpréter comme un commentaire mordant et ironique sur la nouvelle liberté dans le design et le combat pour la survie dans le Japon surpeuplé.

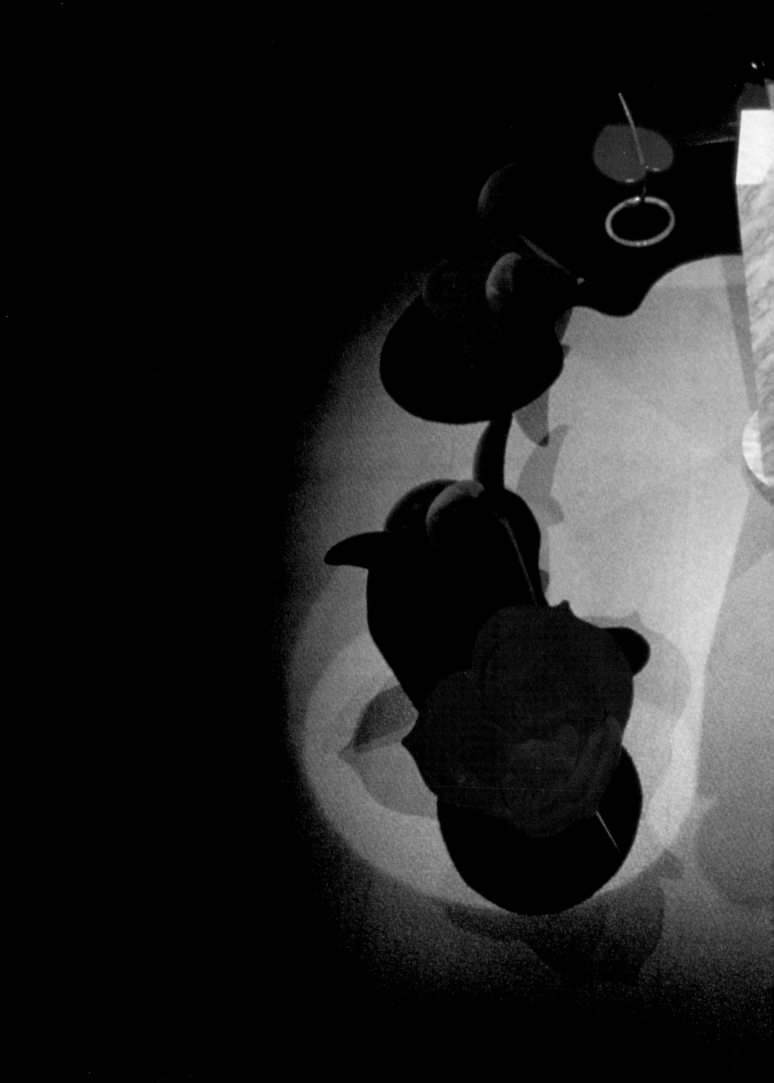

p.50
Anthurium, 1990
Beistelltisch, side table, table basse

Getsuen, 1990
Sessel, armchair, fauteuil

p.48/49
I Fiori, 1990
Polstermöbel, upholstered furniture,
meubles rembourrés

Rose Chair, 1991
Sessel, armchair, fauteuil

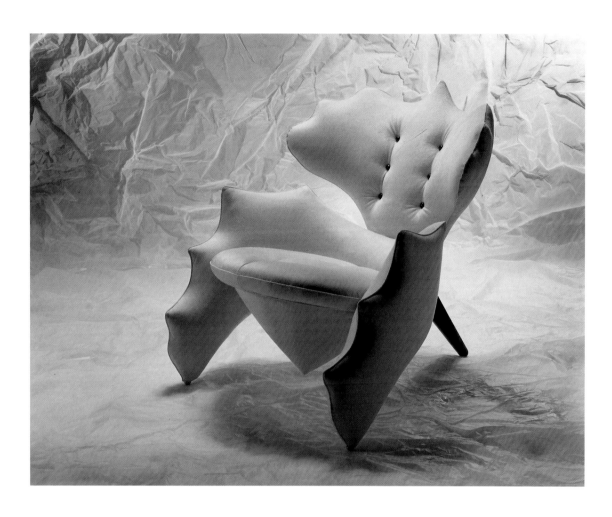

Orchid, 1991
Sessel, armchair, fauteuil

天 _cielo_
無 _nulla_
命 _vita_
悲 _tristezza_

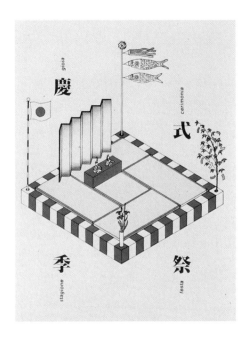

慶 _gioia_
式 _cerimonia_
季 _stagione_
祭 _festa_

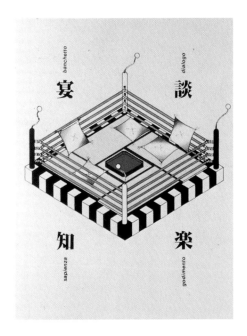

宴 _banchetto_
談 _dialogo_
知 _sapienza_
楽 _godimento_

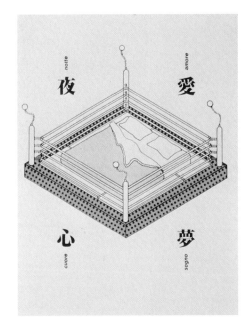

夜 _notte_
愛 _amore_
心 _cuore_
夢 _sogno_

Memphis Tawaray, 1981
Bett, bed, lit
Zeichnungen, drawings, dessins

Memphis Tawaraya, 1981
Bett, bed, lit

Xspace, 1989
Damentoilette/Herrentoilette, »Women«/»Men«,
W.C. Dames/Messieurs

p. 56
Xspace, 1989
Sanitärschrank, bathroom cabinet, armoire de toilette

Tomato Bank, 1989
Tamashima, Kurashiki City, Okaya

Yamato, 1986
Kimono Shop, Yokohama

Gore-Tex Japan, 1990
Empfangshalle, reception hall, foyer d'accueil
Akazutsumi, Tokyo

SHIRO KURAMATA

SHIRO KURAMATA

1934	Geboren in Tokio
1953	Diplom an der Kunsthochschule Tokio
1956	Diplom an der Kuwasawa Design Schule in Tokio
1965	Gründung des Kuramata Design Büros in Tokio
1981	Japanischer Kulturpreis
1981-83	Mitarbeit bei Memphis in Mailand
1991	gestorben

1934	Born in Tokyo
1953	Diploma from Tokyo Art College
1956	Diploma from Kuwasawa Design School, Tokyo
1965	Establishes Kuramata Design Bureau, Tokyo
1981	Japanese Prize for the Arts
1981-83	Works for Memphis in Milan
1991	Dies

1934	Naît à Tokyo
1953	Diplôme de la Faculté des Beaux-Arts de Tokyo
1956	Diplôme de l'Ecole de Design Kuwasawa à Tokyo
1965	Fondation du bureau de Design Kuramata à Tokyo
1981	Prix de la Culture japonaise
1981-83	Travail chez Memphis à Milan
1991	Décès

Shiro Kuramata war der größte und einflußreichste Gestalter des modernen Japan, ein Poet der kreativen Leere, der die westliche Bauhaus-Moderne mit surrealistischen und minimalistischen Elementen anreicherte und auf das östliche Denken übertrug. Seine Boutiquen und Restaurant-Interieurs in aller Welt haben eine ganze Designergeneration beeinflußt. Kuramata wollte funktionale Zwänge durch das Spiel überwinden. Seine entmaterialisierten Entwürfe verharren in einem esoterischen Schwebezustand, aber sie sind zugleich voller Präsenz und Sinnlichkeit. Er spitzt das Spannungsverhältnis von Funktion und Form zu, bis es kurz vor dem Auseinanderbrechen steht. An seinem Lieblingsmaterial Plexiglas schätzte er die Ambiguität, daß es kalt wie Glas und warm wie Holz ist. Er goß Rosen in Flüssigglas ein, damit sie ewig blühen. Seine transparenten Metallmöbel scheinen zu schweben. Sie strahlen eine sensorische Imaginationskraft aus und übertragen die synästhetischen Wahrnehmungen der heutigen postindustriellen Mediengesellschaft ins Design. Auch moderne Möbelklassiker hat Kuramata durch Neuinterpretation entgegenständlicht.

Shiro Kuramata was the greatest and most influential designer in modern Japan. A true poet of creative vacancy, he added surreal and minimalist elements to western Bauhaus Modernism and adapted this to oriental ways of thinking. His boutiques and restaurant interiors around the world have influenced a whole generation of designers. Kuramata's aim was to use games-playing to overcome functional necessities. His de-materialized designs are in a state of esoteric suspension, yet they are sensuously present. He heightens tensions of function and form till it seems something ought to give. What he liked about his favourite material, perspex, was its ambiguity: cold as glass yet warm as wood. He cast roses in glass so that they would flower forever. His transparent metal furniture seems almost to be floating; it emanates sensory imaginative power, and introduces the synaesthetic perceptions of today's post-industrial media society into design. Kuramata's new interpretations also de-objectified modern furniture classics.

Shiro Kuramata a été le plus grand et le plus influent styliste du Japon moderne, un poète du vide créatif qui a enrichi les théories modernes du Bauhaus occidental d'éléments surréalistes et minimalistes et les a propagées dans le système de pensée asiatique. Ses décorations de boutiques et de restaurants dans le monde entier ont influencé toute une génération de designers. Kuramata voulait vaincre les contraintes fonctionnelles par le jeu. Ses créations dématérialisées restent en suspens dans un état de flottement ésotérique, mais elles sont en même temps remplies de vie et de sensualité. Il porte à son comble, presque jusqu'à la fêlure, la tension qui relie la fonction et la forme. Sa préférence allait au plexiglas dont il appréciait l'ambiguïté: chaud comme le bois, froid comme le verre. Ses roses enrobées de verre fleurissent à jamais. Ses meubles de métal transparents semblent flotter, on y sent une puissance créative œuvrant au niveau des sensations, et leurs formes reflètent les perceptions synesthésiques de notre société médiatisée post-industrielle. Kuramata a également désobjectisé des classiques modernes du meuble en leur donnant une nouvelle interprétation.

Solaris, 1977
Kommode, sideboard, commode

p. 67
Furniture in irregular forms, 1970
Schubladenschrank, chest of drawers,
armoire à tiroirs

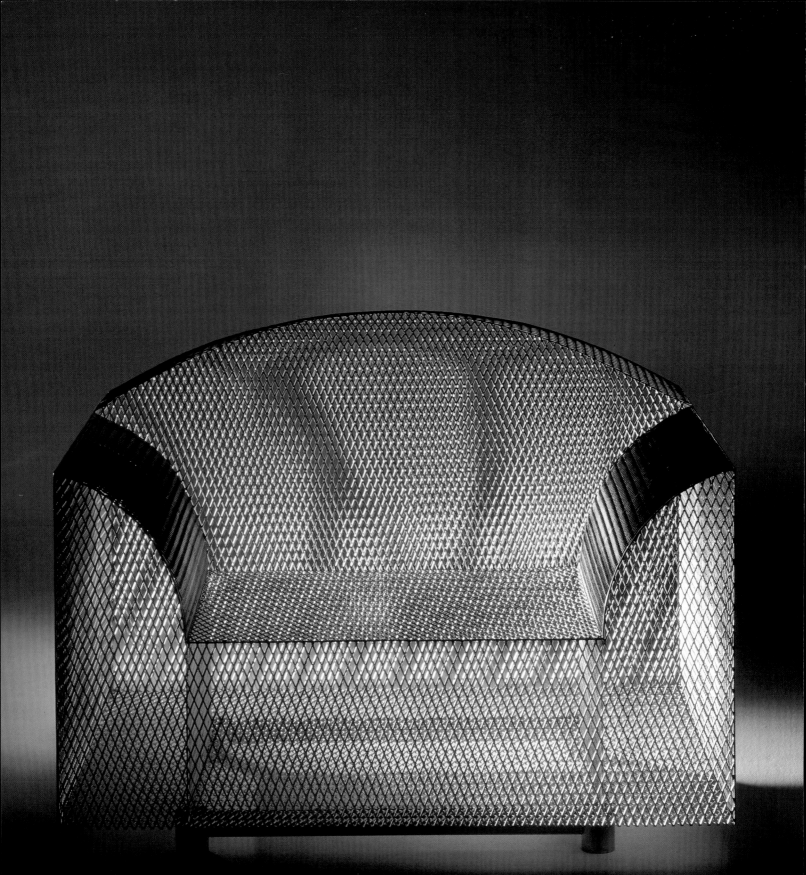

Vol. 2 - Hommage to Josef Hoffmann, 1986
Sessel, armchair, fauteuil

p. 68
How High The Moon, 1986
Sessel, armchair, fauteuil

Sing Sing Sing, 1985
Stuhl, chair, chaise

Koko, 1985
Hocker, stool, tabouret

Begin the Beguine - Hommage to Josef Hoffmann, 1985
Stuhl, chair, chaise

Copacabana, 1988
Handtasche, handbag, sac à main

p. 72
Hydrogen Dream, 1988
Leuchte, lamp, lampe

Miss Blanche, 1988
Sessel, armchair, fauteuil

Bar Restaurant Comblé, 1988
Shizuoka

p. 77
Spiral, 1990
Hocker aus der »Spiral«-Boutique,
stool from the »Spiral« boutique,
tabouret de la boutique «Spiral», Tokyo

p. 78 / 79
Spiral Interior, 1990
Boutique für Einrichtungsgegenstände,
boutique for interior design decor,
boutique pour aménagement d'intérieur, Tokyo

Bar БАР, 1989

p. 81
Bar БАР, 1989

Boutique Issey Miyake Men, 1987
Shibuya, Seibu Tokyo

Sushi Bar, 1988
Kiyotomo

ATSUSHI KITAGAWARA

ATSUSHI KITAGAWARA

1950	Geboren in Tokio
1977	Diplom an der Architekturfakultät der Kunsthochschule Tokio
1980	Gründung eines eigenen Architekturbüros
1990	Gastprofessor an der Waseda-Universität
1991	Preis des »Japan Institute of Architects« für junge Architekten

1950	Born in Tokyo
1977	Diploma from the School of Architecture, Tokyo Art College
1980	Establishes his own architecture bureau
1990	Visiting professor at Waseda University
1991	Receives the Japan Institute of Architects' prize for young architects

1950	Naît à Tokyo
1977	Diplôme de la Faculté d'architecture de l'Université des Beaux-Arts de Tokyo
1980	Fondation d'un bureau d'architecture indépendant
1990	Professeur libre à l'Université Waseda
1991	Prix du «Japan Institute of Architects» attribué aux jeunes architectes

Schneidende bis verletzende Silhouetten, aufgeplatzte Häuser wie das berühmte »Rise«-Kino in Tokio und die Kollisionsästhetik von deformierten Möbeln machen Atsushi Kitagawara zum Katastrophenphilosophen unter den neuen japanischen Designern. Bei aller Gefährlichkeit haben die Entwürfe stark sensualistische Züge und provozieren die Berührung geradezu. Kitagawara will die bislang als fremde Übermacht empfundene Technik mit dem Menschen versöhnen und geht dabei, etwa bei seinem Regal »Veldi« mit seinen dreidimensionalen Verformungen, auch handwerklich an die Grenzen des Machbaren. Im Zeitalter der technisch simulierten Erfahrungen gilt Kitagawara als »Realist« unter den Erfindern, weil er den immateriellen Schocks und Sensationen eine materielle Grundlage gibt.

Outlines so sharp as to be cutting, exploded buildings such as the famed Rise Cinema in Tokyo, and the collision aesthetics of malformed furniture – all these have made Atsushi Kitagawara the disaster philosopher among younger Japanese designers. Dangerous though they are, his designs are strongly sensuous and tempt us to touch. Till now, technology has been seen as an alien and superior power, but Kitagawara is out to reconcile us to it, and in the process – in his »Veldi« shelving, say, with its three-dimensional malformations – he touches the limits of what it is physically possible to make. In an age of technically simulated experience, Kitagawara is seen as the realist among contemporary inventors, because he provides a material foundation for the shocks and sensations of a non-material nature.

Les silhouettes coupantes, blessantes des créations de Atsushi Kitagawara, ses bâtiments éclatés, comme le célèbre cinéma «Rise» de Tokyo, et ses meubles déformés à l'esthétisme heurtant font de lui le philosophe des catastrophes parmi les nouveaux designers japonais. Malgré leur aspect «dangereux», toutes ces œuvres sont empreintes d'une forte sensualité et provoquent l'émotion. Kitagawara veut réconcilier la technique, ressentie jusqu'ici comme une puissance supérieure étrangère, avec l'homme, et son étagère «Veldi» aux déformations tridimensionnelles montre qu'il est arrivé, et cela également au niveau de l'artisanat, aux limites de ce qui peut se faire. A l'ère des expérimentations simulées techniquement, Kitagawara, qui donne une base matérielle aux chocs immatériels et aux sensations, est considéré comme le «réaliste» entre les inventeurs.

Veldi, 1988
Regal, shelf, étagère

Paphomet, 1988
Kommode, sideboard, commode

Goldberg, 1988
Tisch mit Glasplatte, table with glass top,
table avec plaque de verre

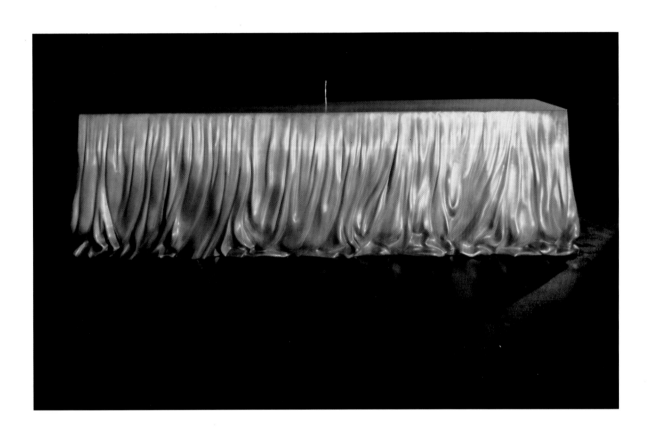

Empfangstisch, reception desk, table de réception, 1989
Edoken Head Office, Tokyo

Daffodil, 1988
Sofa, sofa, canapé

Vasara, 1989
Juwelier, jeweller, bijoutier

Vasara, 1989
Juwelier, jeweller, bijoutier

SHIGERU UCHIDA

SHIGERO UCHIDA

1943	Geboren in Yokohama
1966	Diplom an der Kuwasawa Design Schule in Tokio
1970	Gründung des Uchida Design Büros
1974-78	Lehrtätigkeit an der Hochschule für Kunst und Design in Tokio
1981	Gründung des Designstudios »Atelier 80« mit seiner Frau Ikuyo Mitsuhashi und Toru Nishioka

1943	Born in Yokohama
1966	Diploma from Kuwasawa Design School, Tokyo
1970	Establishes Uchida Design Office
1974-78	Teaching at Tokyo College of Art and Design
1981 his	Establishes »Atelier 80« design studio with wife, Ikuyo Mitsuhashi, and Toru Nishioka

1943	Naît à Yokohama
1966	Diplôme de l'Ecole de Design de Kuwasawa à Tokyo
1970	Création du bureau de Design Uchida
1974-78	Maître de conférences à l'Université des Beaux-Arts et du Design de Tokyo
1981	Fondation du studio de design «Atelier 80» avec sa femme Ikuyo Mitsuhashi et Toru Nishioka

Für einen der einflußreichsten Traditionalisten des neuen japanischen Designs haben Shigeru Uchidas Entwürfe enorm modernistische bis futuristische Züge. Ihr Bezug zur alten japanischen Gestaltung ist eher intellektuell denn formal. Uchida geht von der shintoistischen Raumauffassung, von »heiligen« und »profanen« Räumen aus und treibt ihre Abstraktheit in seinen Möbeln und Interieurs noch weiter. Seine Objekte erinnern an Stelen und Totems, seine Inneneinrichtungen für Rei-Kawakubo- und Yamamoto-Boutiquen dramatisieren den Raum durch tempelartige Säulenreihen oder hervorspringende Stahlwände. Uchida ist ein sensibler Dialektiker, der Bewegungselemente und Statik, intime und offene Zonen, Kunststoffe und Naturmaterialien paart. Sein dreibeiniger Dreieckstuhl »September« von 1981 mit dreieckiger Sitzfläche und umlaufender, halbrunder Lehne erinnert an Philippe Starck, entstand aber lange vor Starcks Entwurf.

For one of the most influential traditionalists in recent Japanese design, Shigeru Uchida's work has decidedly Modernist and even Futurist traits. Its relation to old-fashioned Japanese design is of a cerebral rather than formal order. Uchida starts from the Shintoist idea of sacred and profane spaces, and pursues this abstraction in his furniture and interiors. His artefacts recall steles and totem poles, while his interiors for the Rei Kawakubo and Yamamoto boutiques dramatize space by using temple-like rows of pillars or buttressed steel walls. Uchida is a subtle dialectician, matching dynamic and static elements, private and public zones, synthetic and natural materials. »September«, his three-legged triangular stool designed in 1981, with a semirounded back may recall Philippe Starck but actually antedates Starck's design by a good while.

Si l'on considère que Shigeru Uchida est l'un des traditionalistes les plus influents du nouveau design japonais, on constate que ses créations ont des traits bien ultramodernes voire futuristes. Leur référence aux anciens agencements japonais est plus intellectuel que formel. Uchida reprend à son compte la perception shintoïste de l'espace qui divise celui-ci en aires «sacrées» et «profanes», et pousse plus loin encore cet idéal d'abstraction dans ses meubles et intérieurs. Ses objets nous font songer aux stèles et aux totems, ses agencements intérieurs pour les boutiques Rei Kawakubo et Yamamoto dramatisent l'espace par des rangées de colonnes dignes d'un temple ou des panneaux de métal faisant saillie. Uchida est un dialecticien doué de sensibilité qui accouple les éléments mobiles et statiques, les zones intimes et ouvertes, les matériaux artificiels et naturels. Sa chaise «septembre» de 1981, qui a trois pieds, un siège triangulaire et un dossier en demi-cercle qui en fait le tour, rappelle Philippe Starck, mais a été conçue bien avant la création de Starck.

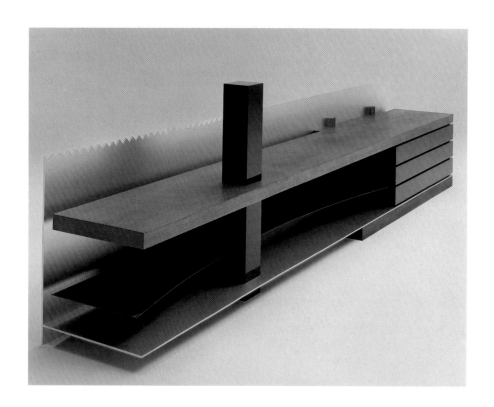

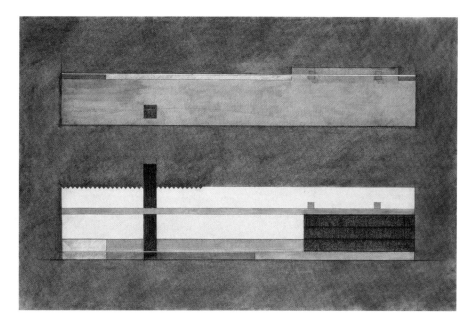

NY Sideboard, 1986
Kommode, sideboard, commode
Zeichnung, drawing, dessin

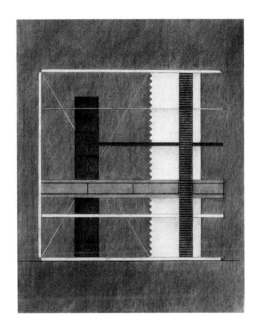

NY Shelf, 1986
Regal, shelf, étagère
Zeichnung, drawing, dessin

Il Tavolo per Aldo, 1989
Tisch, table
Zeichnung, drawing, dessin

L'Armadio per Aldo, 1989
Kommode, sideboard, commode
Zeichnung, drawing, dessin

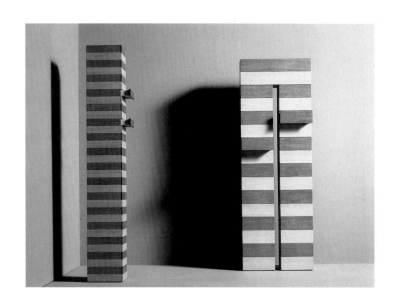

Kagu, 1991
Kommode, sideboard, commode
Kommode (quadratisch), sideboard (square), commode (carrée)
Schrank, cabinet, armoire

p. 107
Dear Morris, 1989
Standuhr, grandfather clock, horloge

Kagu-T.D.W.Chair, 1989
Stuhl, chair, chaise
Design Ikuyo Mitsuhashi

August, 1989
Stuhl, chair, chaise

Kagu, 1991
Regal (farbig), shelf (coloured), étagère (en couleurs)

p. 111
Kagu, 1991
Regal (weiß), shelf (white), étagère (blanche)

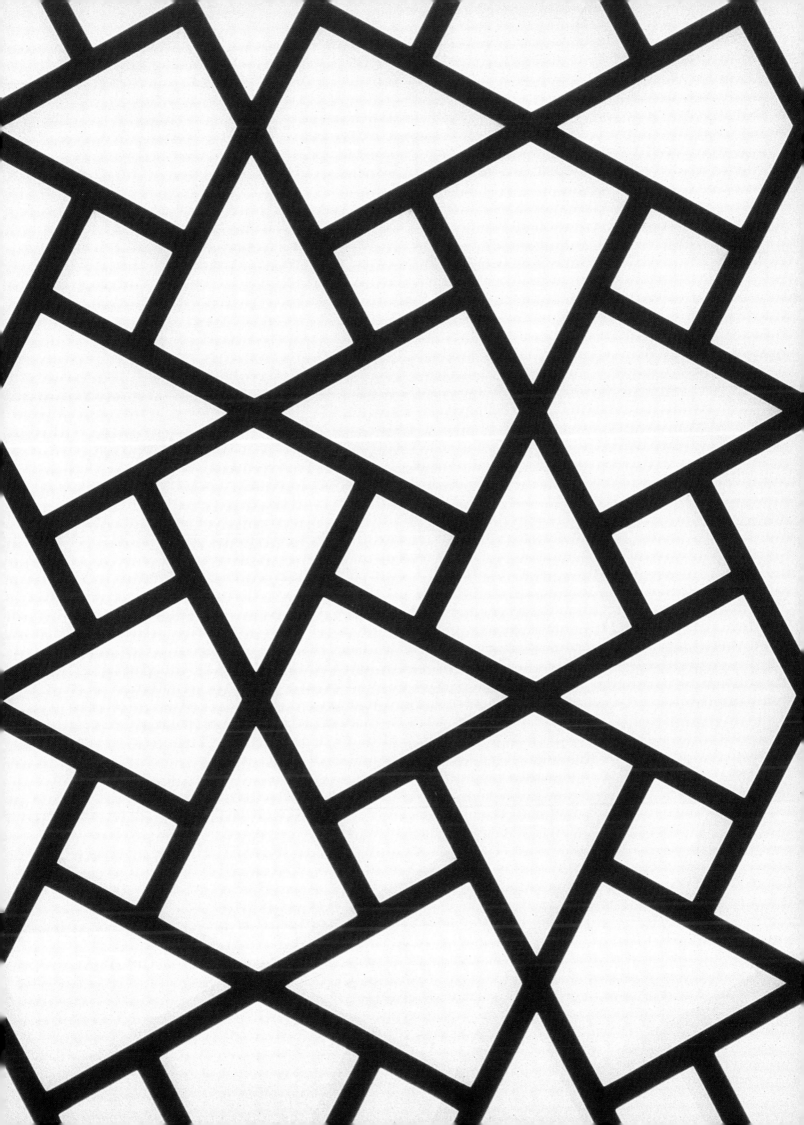

HIGH TECH

Die große Erfindungsgabe der Japaner, so heißt es, ist durch soziale Notwendigkeiten entstanden. So wie die komplizierte Kanji-Schrift zunächst nicht elektronisch kodierbar war und deshalb die analoge Übertragung per Faksimile erfunden werden mußte, so läßt sich auch die Weltneuheit des Walkman aus der extremen Überbevölkerung der japanischen Großstädte erklären, in denen sich die Bewohner mittels Kopfhörern akustische Privatzonen schaffen wollten. Auch die Multifunktionalität der Technikprodukte ist auf die erzwungene Raumökonomie zurückzuführen, möglichst viele Anwendungen auf kleinster Fläche unterzubringen. Auffällig ist, daß japanische Geräte keine häßlichen Rück- oder Unteransichten haben, sondern stets nach allen Seiten hin wohlgeformt sind. Den ergonomischen Ansatz europäischer Gestalter haben die Japaner zu einer abstrakt-organischen Ästhetik weiterentwickelt. Je komplizierter die Gerätefunktionen werden und je stärker die Technik durch Miniaturisierung zurücktritt, desto freier werden neuere Entwürfe. Für extrem dünne Flüssigkristallbildschirme oder für Computerterminals werden anschauliche Gegenwerte geschaffen, die entweder nostalgische Elemente der fünfziger Jahre oder sogar primitivistische Formen aufgreifen. Durch gesteigerte Produktion in Kleinserien haben Designer größeren Spielraum, Erfindungen nicht umständlich zu erforschen, sondern direkt am Markt auszuprobieren. Was die Italiener Anfang der achtziger Jahre im Möbeldesign mit gefühlsbetonten Entwürfen begonnen hatten, übertragen die Japaner heute auf die Technik. Die Geräte sollen immer imaginativer und emotionaler wirken.

It is often said that the great Japanese talent for invention is a product of social necessity. Just as the complex Kanji script initially defied electronic encoding and thus necessitated the invention of facsimile (FAX) transfer, so too the novel Walkman originated in the extreme overcrowding of Japanese cities, where headphones allowed individuals to establish their own acoustic privacy. The multifunctionality of tech products also derives from spatial economies. As many uses as possible have to be catered for in as confined an area as possible. It is striking that Japanese gadgets lack an ugly reverse or under side; they are attractive whichever side shows. The ergonomic tendencies in certain European designers have been taken further by the Japanese, towards an aesthetic of organic abstraction. The more complex the functions of gadgets grow, and the more technology is displaced by miniaturization, the more untrammelled the new designs are becoming. Extremely thin liquid crystal screens, or state-of-the-art computer terminals, come with features that are easy on the eye, either with a nostalgic 1950s flavour or with something even more fundamental. By increasing production in small series, designers win greater leeway to dispense with research on inventions: instead, they can be tested in the market place. What the Italians initiated with their emotional furniture designs in the early 1980s, the Japanese are now extending into tech. Gadgetry now has to have an ever more imaginative and emotional impact.

On dit que la grande créativité des Japonais est née des nécessités sociales. L'écriture Kanji, si compliquée qu'elle ne pouvait être codée électroniquement, conduisit à l'invention du transfert analogue par facsimilé, et la nouveauté mondiale qu'est le baladeur s'explique quand on connaît l'extrême surpopulation des métropoles japonaises, où les écouteurs permettent aux gens de se créer leurs propres territoires acoustiques. La polyvalence des produits techniques trouve également sa source dans l'économie au niveau de l'espace qui oblige à rendre la plus petite surface utilisable de toutes les façons possibles. Il est frappant que les appareils japonais ne présentent pas de face antérieure ou de dessous moins présentable, mais soient au contraire bien faits sur toutes leurs faces. Les Japonais ont repris l'idée de départ ergonomique des concepteurs européens pour en faire une esthétique organico-abstraite. Et les nouvelles conceptions se libèrent dans la mesure où les fonctions des appareils deviennent compliquées, et où la technique se miniaturise. On crée pour des écrans à cristaux liquides extrêmement minces ou pour des consoles d'ordinateur des équivalents expressifs s'inspirant soit de la nostalgie des années 50, soit même de formes primitives. Grâce à la production accrue en petites séries, les stylistes ont maintenant la liberté de tester directement leurs inventions sur le marché au lieu de leur faire subir des analyses compliquées. Les Japonais reportent aujourd'hui sur la technique ce que les concepteurs de mobilier italiens avaient commencé à faire au début des années 80 avec leurs créations sentimentales. Les appareils doivent être toujours plus ingénieux et leur charge émotionnelle plus puissante.

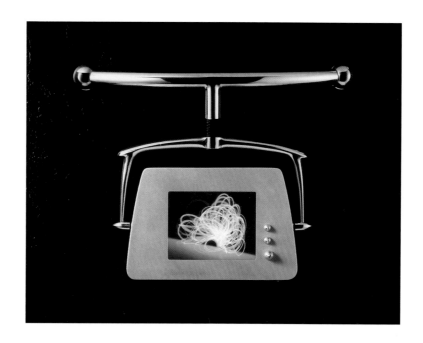

Liquid Crystal Museum, 1992
LCD Superflach-Bildschirm,
LCD ultra flat screen,
écran LCD ultraplat

Design Sharp

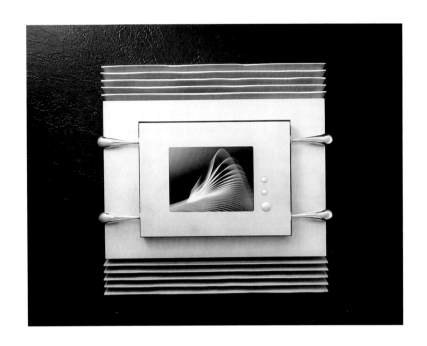

Liquid Crystal Museum, 1992
LCD Superflach-Bildschirm,
LCD ultra flat screen,
écran LCD ultraplat

Design Sharp

PSO Terminal, 1989
Elektronische Registrierkasse, electronic cash register,
caisse enregistreuse électronique

Design Maxinart

p.116
Video-shell, 1989
Videorekorder, video cassette recorder, magnétoscope

Design Shintaro Tanaka

Carna, 1989
Rollstuhl, wheelchair, fauteuil roulant

Design Kazuo Kawasaki

S-Cargo, 1989
Kleintransporter, Mini-van, camionnette

Design Nissan

Nissan Boga, 1989
Autointerior, dashboard, habitacle

Design   Nissan

Nissan Boga, 1989
Auto, car, voiture

Design Nissan

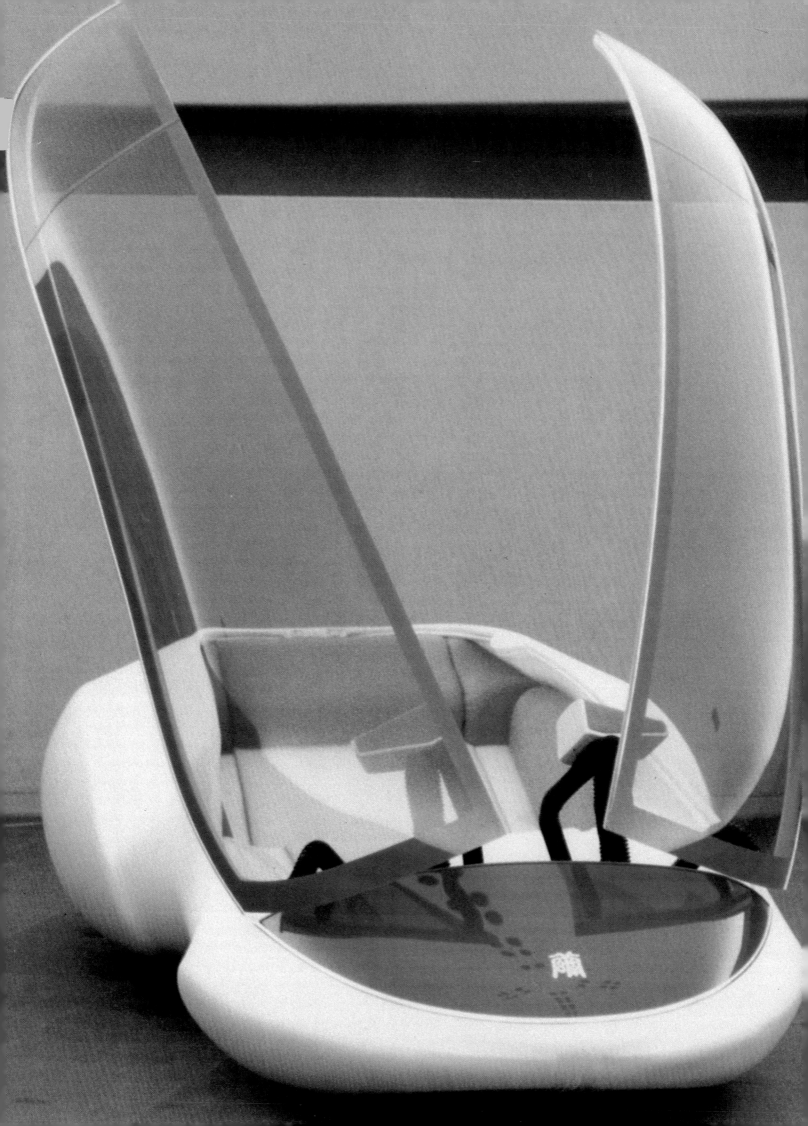

Atode-Car, 1990
Modelle aus den Designstudios von Toyota
Drafts of designs from Toyota's design studios
Etudes des studios de design de Toyota

Das japanische Retro-Design ist die vielleicht extremste Ausgeburt des heutigen Fin de siècle. In einer Überflußgesellschaft kultivieren die Retro-Designer die Kunst, kleinste Marktlücken zu entdecken. Sie haben junge, wohlhabende Käufer im Auge, die nicht nur Waren, sondern Botschaften kaufen wollen. Die Entwürfe schlachten historische Images und emotionelle Erinnerungswerte aus, etwa alte Reporter-Kameras aus Hitchcocks Hollywood-Filmen oder Fahrzeugkarosserien aus Fellinis Rom. Um sich von der Massenproduktion abzusetzen, werden Retro-Entwürfe oft nur in Kleinauflagen hergestellt. Die Produkte müssen von den Kunden entweder lange vorbestellt werden oder sind zuweilen nur durch Verlosung erhältlich. Beim Nissan »Figaro« gab es eine dreistufige Lotterie, bei der jedesmal achttausend Wagen verlost wurden. Die Warteliste umfaßte Mitte 1991 rund 210 000 Käufer. Die Retro-Ästhetik ist nicht typisch für das heutige japanische Design. Aber sie zeigt, wie angesichts einer überstylten Umwelt und eines saturierten Publikums noch neue Firmen-Images und Käufergelüste erzeugt werden können.

Japanese Retro Design is arguably the most extreme of the current fin de siècle phenomena. In a society of surfeit, Retro designers are cultivating the art of discovering the smallest possible gaps in the market. They target young, well-to-do consumers who buy not just the goods but also the message. The designs exploit historical images and emotional, nostalgic charges – old reporters' cameras, as seen in Hitchcock films, or car bodywork from Fellini's Rome. Retro designs stand out from mass production by being frequently created in small runs. The products either have to be ordered well in advance by clients, or else are occasionally only available by lot. For the Nissan Figaro there was a three-stage lottery with eight thousand cars being given away in each stage. In 1991, there were 210,000 buyers on the waiting list. Retro aesthetics are untypical of contemporary Japanese design, but they do indicate how new company images and buyer wishes can be created in a world saturated with style and for consumers long since sated.

Le rétro-design japonaise est peut-être l'apparition la plus extrême de cette «fin de siècle». Dans une société où règne la surabondance, les rétro-designers cultivent l'art de s'insérer dans les plus petits créneaux du marché. Ils ciblent les acheteurs jeunes et aisés, sensibles au message du produit. Leurs créations exploitent des images historiques et des émotions passées, on retrouve par exemple les vieilles caméras des reporters de Hitchcock ou les carosseries de voitures de Rome de Fellini. Pour se démarquer de la production de masse, les produits rétro ne sont souvent fabriqués qu'en série limitée. Ils doivent avoir fait l'objet d'une commande préalable, ou ne sont parfois accessibles que par tirage au sort. Le Nissan Figaro a fait l'objet d'une loterie à trois niveaux, huit mille voitures ont chaque fois été tirées au sort. En 1991 la liste d'attente comptait 210.000 acheteurs. L'esthétique rétro n'est pas caractéristique du design japonais actuel. Mais elle montre comment il est possible, face à un environnement hyperstylisé et un public saturé, de générer de nouvelles images et de créer de nouveaux besoins.

Nissan Figaro, 1991
Auto, car, voiture

Design Nissan

Nissan Figaro, 1991
Autointerieur, dashboard, habitacle

Design Nissan

Scooter-Frog, 1992
Motorroller, motor-scooter, scooter

Design Yamaha

SW-1, 1991
Motorrad, motorcycle, moto

Design Suzuki

Olympus O-Product, 1988
Autofokus-Kamera, auto-focus camera, caméra autofocus

Design Naoki Sakai

QT-50, 1986
Radiorekorder, radio cassette-recorder, radio-cassette

Design Sharp

AD-1, 1990
Hifi-Stereo Anlage, Hifi stereo unit, chaîne Hifi

Design Fumi Masuda

PRODUCTS

Der extrem schnelle Produktwechsel auf dem japanischen Markt macht es fast unmöglich, Produkt- und Firmen-Images zu entwickeln. Doch aus der Flut der Konsumgüter tauchen immer wieder Objekte auf, die zeitlos wirken. Sie verzichten auf jede illusionistische Ornamentik und sind rundplastisch durchgeformt. Vom einfachen Eßgeschirr in der Tradition der lackierten Holzarbeiten bis zum futuristischen Kinderwagen besitzen die durchweg aus stereometrischen Grundformen komponierten Entwürfe eine hochabstrakte Eleganz. Die Weiterentwicklung konzentriert sich mehr auf formale denn funktionale Aspekte. Es sind überwiegend ästhetische Innovationen, die den Objekten aber nicht appliziert werden, sondern sich wie von innen heraus zu entwickeln scheinen. Alle nicht-technischen Waren verzichten ausdrücklich auf jedes Maschinendesign zugunsten einer wärmeren, mehr körperlichen Gestaltung.

The extremely rapid turnover of products on the Japanese market renders the development of product and company images almost impossible. From the flood of consumer commodities, however, items do repeatedly appear that seem timeless. They dispense with illusionist ornamentation and are moulded in a rounded, sculptural way. From simple crockery in the tradition of wooden lacquerware to futuristic prams, these stereometrical designs have a highly abstract elegance of their own. Evolution then concentrates on formal rather than functional aspects. These innovations are mainly of an aesthetic nature; they are not so much applied to the objects as seem to have developed from within them. All non-technical products expressly dis-pense with machine-made design in favour of warmer, more organic and physical moulding.

Les produits vont et viennent si rapidement sur le marché japonais qu'il est presque impossible de leur créer une image de marque. Mais de nouveaux objets, qui semblent hors du temps, se distinguent dans ce flot de produits de consommation. Ils renoncent à toute ornementation illusoire et adoptent une plastique sans arêtes vives. Qu'il s'agisse de couverts dans la tradition des bois laqués ou de la voiture d'enfant futuriste, les créations, basées généralement sur des formes stéréométriques, possèdent une élégance très abstraite. L'évolution va dans le sens de la forme plus que dans celui de la fonction. Les innovations sont surtout esthétiques, mais elles ne sont pas appliquées aux objets, elles paraissent se développer à partir de l'intérieur. Les articles non techniques renoncent à tout design mécanique au profit d'une forme plus chaude, plus corporelle.

Vittel, 1991
Mineralwasser Flasche, 1,5 Liter, Variante B
Bottle for mineral water, 1.5 litre, version B
Bouteille d'eau minérale, 1,5 litre, type B

Design Masayuki Kurokawa

p.139
Vittel, 1991
Mineralwasser Flasche, 1,5 Liter, Variante A
Bottle for mineral water, 1.5 litre, version A
Bouteille d'eau minérale, 1,5 litre, type A

Design Masayuki Kurokawa

p. 136 / 137
Push Pin, 1986
Reißzwecken, drawing pins, punaises

Design Masayuki Kurokawa

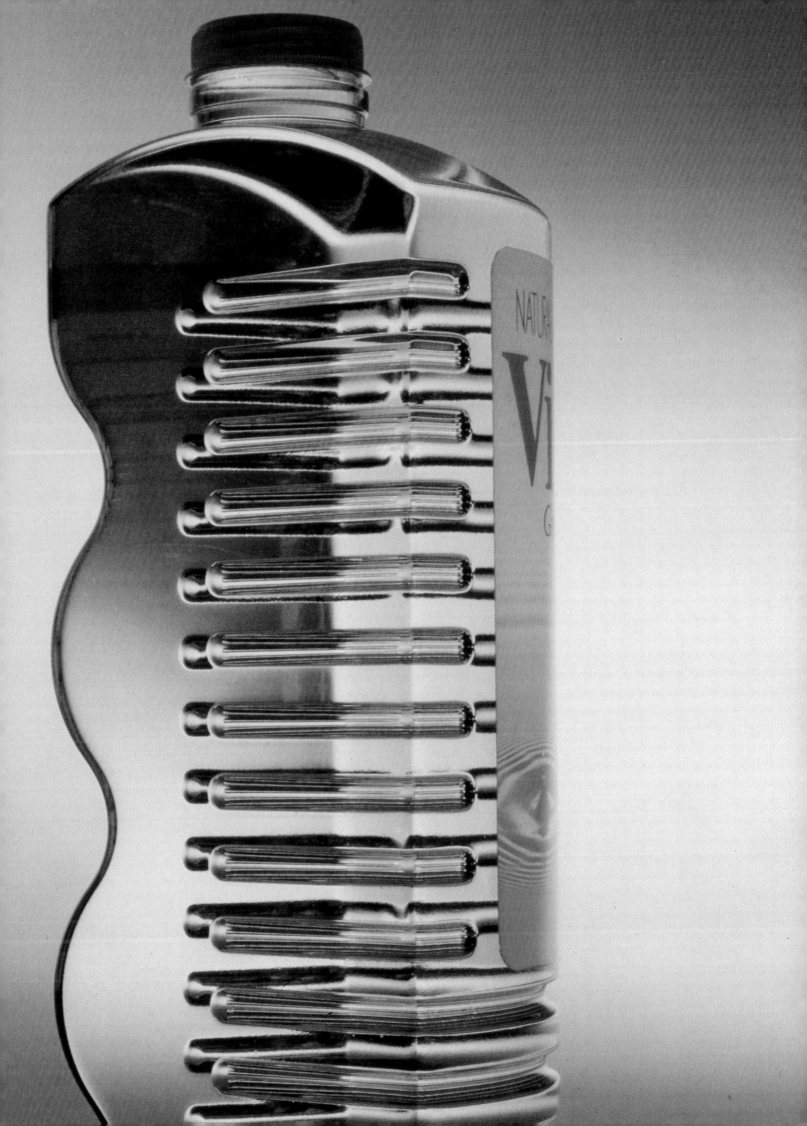

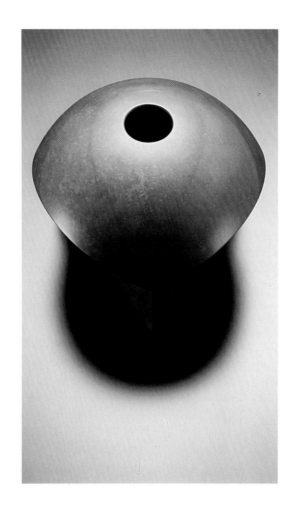

En Series, 1989
Kerzenhalter, candle holder, chandelier

Design Masayuki Kurokawa

En Series Table-Tops, 1989

Design Masayuki Kurokawa

p. 141
En Series, 1989
Blumenvase, flower vase, vase

Design Masayuki Kurokawa

Loppie, 1985
Leuchte, lamp, lampe

Design Hisako Watanabe

p. 143
Oshiris, 1989
Leuchte, lamp, lampe

Design Kenji Oki

Umeda Stand, 1986
Bodenleuchte, floor lamp, luminaire

Design Masanori Umeda

p. 144
Doping Lamp, 1988
Leuchte, lamp, lampe

Design Guen Bertheau-Suzuki

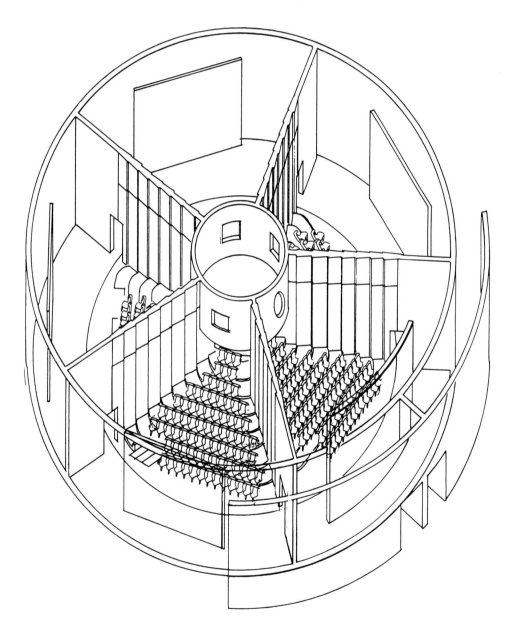

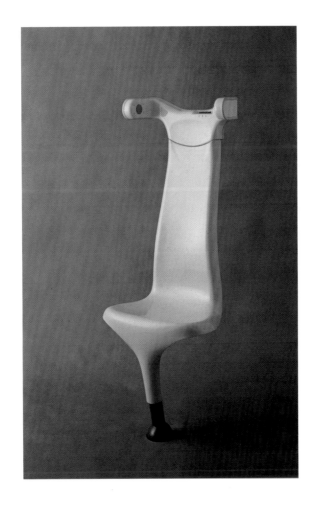

Multi Lingual Chair, 1992
Stuhl mit integrierter Übersetzungsanlage
für das drehbare Auditorium im japanischen Pavillon, Expo Sevilla
Chair with integrated translation system
for the revolving auditorium in the Japanese Pavilion, Expo Sevilla
Chaise avec traduction intégrée
pour l'auditorium tournant au pavillon japonaise, Expo Séville

Design Toshiyuki Kita

p. 146
Drehbares Auditorium, revolving auditorium, auditorium tournant, 1992
Japanischer Pavillion, Expo Sevilla
Japanese Pavilion, Expo Sevilla
Pavillon japonais, Expo Séville
Zeichnung, drawing, dessin

Design Toshiyuki Kita

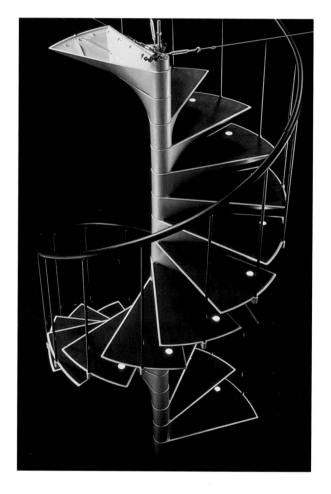

Aica, 1991
Wendeltreppe, spiral staircase, escalier tournant

Design Masayuki Kurokawa

FURNITURE

Wegen ihrer ausgeprägten Kultur des Fußbodens verfügen die Japaner über keine vergleichbare Möbeltradition wie der Westen. Aufgrund der Kargheit der alten Interieurs ist die Weiterentwicklung traditioneller Einrichtungsgegenstände auf kontinuierliche Verbesserung beschränkt. Neue Möbelentwürfe dagegen, wie Tische, Stühle und Bänke, die im traditionellen japanischen Wohnhaus nicht vorkommen, entfalten um so größeren Gestaltungsreichtum. Hier werden direkt europäische Entwicklungen von der frühen Moderne bis zu Memphis aufgegriffen und mit japanischem Feingefühl neu interpretiert. Wo völlig neue Objekte frei von formalen und funktionalen Vorbildern entworfen werden, entstehen skulpturale bis raumkünstlerische Installationen. Sie suchen einen neuen, dritten Weg zwischen der westlichen und östlichen Tradition.

Because of their floor culture, the Japanese lack any furniture tradition that could be compared with that of the West. Given the spartan look of old-style interiors, the options for the further development and improvement of traditional ideas are limited. In the case of new kinds of furniture not found in a conventional Japanese home – such as tables, chairs and benches – designers are all the more fertile in their ideas. European lines from the early modern period through to Memphis are seized upon and re-interpreted with Japanese sensitivity. Where completely new artefacts are designed independently of formal or functional models, installations of a sculptural or spatial/artistic nature tend to result. The Japanese are seeking a new third way between the western and oriental traditions.

Les Japonais, et cela est dû à l'importance du sol au niveau culturel, n'ont pas de tradition d'ameublement comparable à celle des Occidentaux. En raison du dépouillement des anciens intérieurs, l'évolution des meubles n'est en fait qu'une amélioration continue. Par contre, les nouvelles créations, telles que les tables, les chaises et les bancs, qu'on ne trouve pas dans le logement japonais traditionnel, manifestent une richesse de formes d'autant plus grande. Ici, on s'inspire des objets créés en Europe depuis le début de l'époque moderne jusqu'à Memphis, et on les réinterprète avec la délicatesse japonaise. Si des modèles fonctionnels et formels font défaut, on voit apparaître des agencements sculpturaux voire des reliefs artistiques. Ces objets sont en quête d'une troisième voie au-delà des traditions occidentales et orientales.

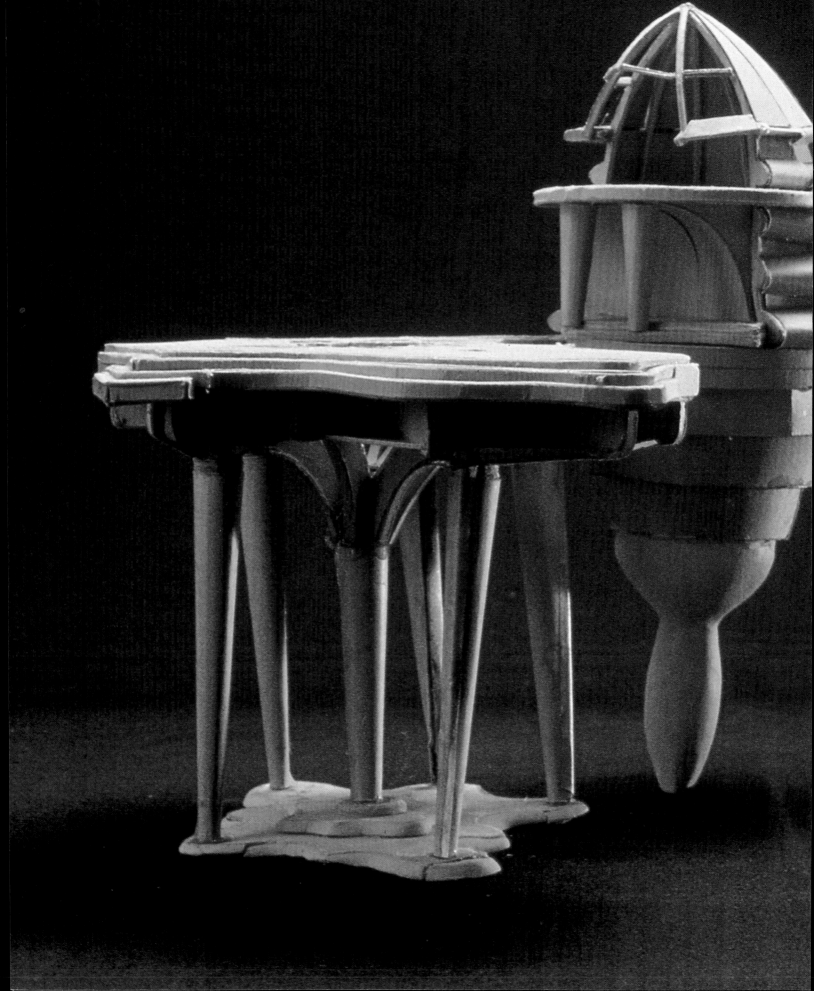

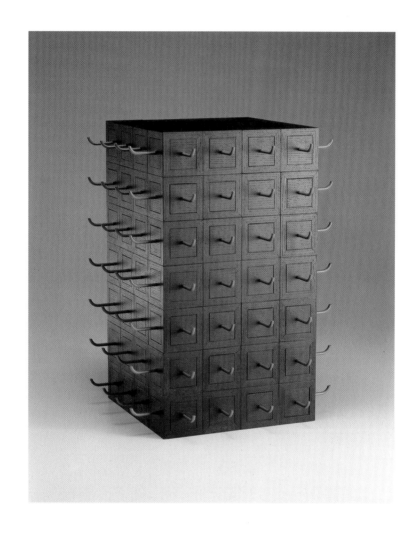

Furniture with Drawers, 1987
Schrank, cabinet, armoire

Design Takashi Kanone

p. 155
Tana System Libro, 1988
Bücherregal, bookcase, bibliothèque

Design Masayuki Kurokawa

p.152 & 153
Mal Chair, Mal Land, 1986
Tisch und Stuhl, table and chair, table et chaise

Design Masaharu Takasaki

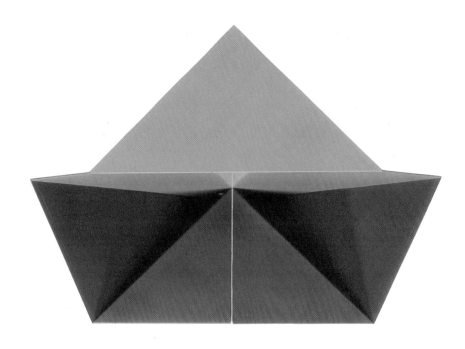

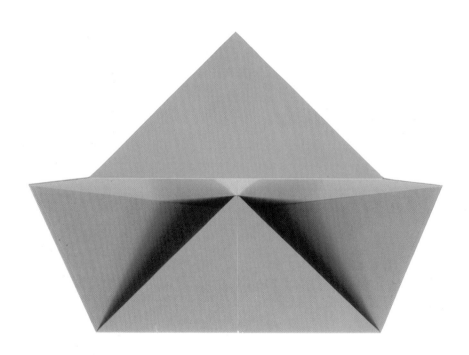

Origami, 1992
Sitzbank, Straßenmöbel aus Stahl
steel bench, street furniture,
banc de rue en acier

Design Hirotoshi Sawada

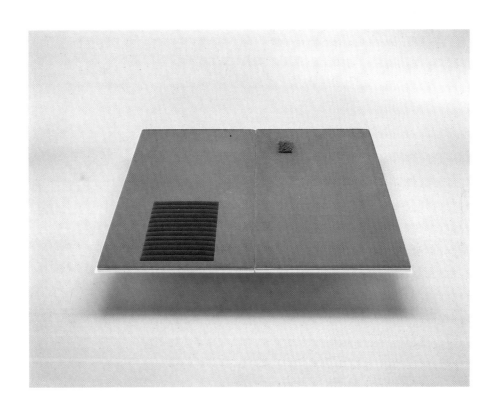

1800 mm square, 1989
Klappbett, folding bed, lit pliant

Design Hirotoshi Sawada

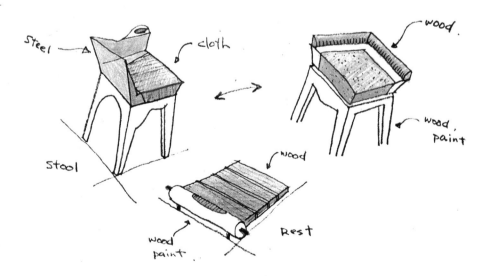

Andy's Stool & Andy's Rest, 1989
Stuhl & Sitzfläche, chair & seating design, chaise & siège
Entwurfszeichnungen, draft drawings, croquis

Design Masanao Arai

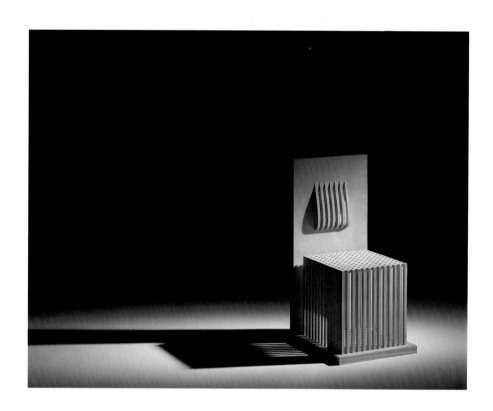

Samurai, 1988
Stuhl, chair, chaise

Design Shuji Hisada

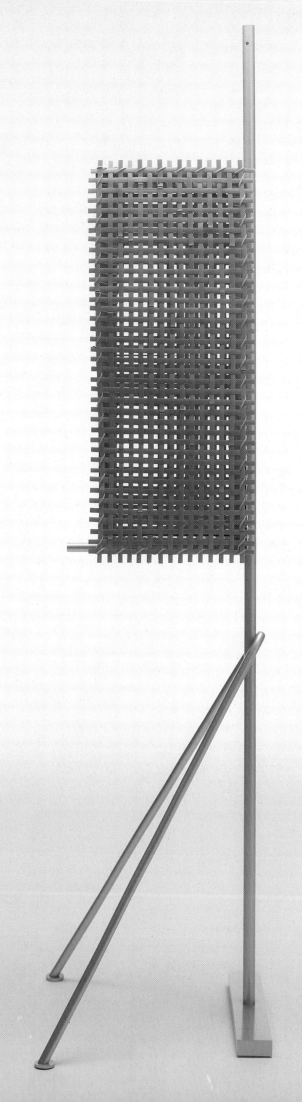

The fragrance of flowers was born on the spring breeze, 1988
Ablage, storage design, étagère

Design Hideo Mori

p. 162
The sound of a violin was born on the wind, 1988
Ablage, storage design, étagère

Design Hideo Mori

The cabinets which are dressed in the blue water color, 1992
Kommode, Vorder- und Rückseite, cabinet, front and back,
commode de face et de dos

Design Hideo Mori

The cabinets which are dressed in the blue water color, 1992
Kommode, sideboard, commode
Entwurfszeichnungen, draft sketches, croquis

Design Hideo Mori

Sea Chair, 1989
Bank, bench, banc

Design Mitsuru Senda

p. 166 & 167
Wink, 1980
Ohrensessel, wing chair, fauteuil à oreilles

Design Toshiyuki Kita

Tube, 1988
Bank, bench, banc

Design Mitsuru Senda

Zofar 1, 1990
Sofa, sofa, canapé

Design Makoto Sei Watanabe

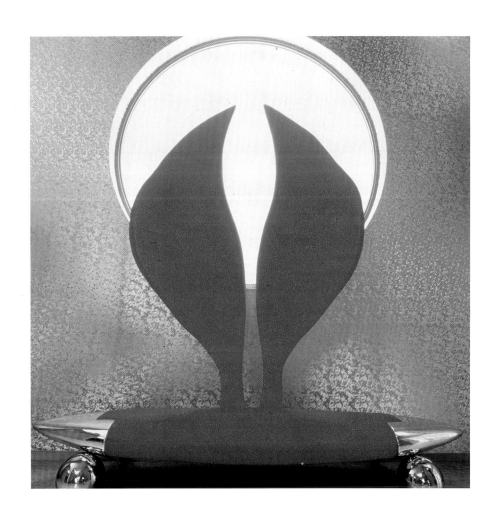

Zofar 2, 1990
Sofa, sofa, canapé

Design Makoto Sei Watanabe

Tokyo Micky Mouse, 1988
Sofa, sofa, canapé

Design Teruaki Ohashi

p.173
Utsly Gutsly, 1991
Sessel, armchair, fauteuil

Design Hironen

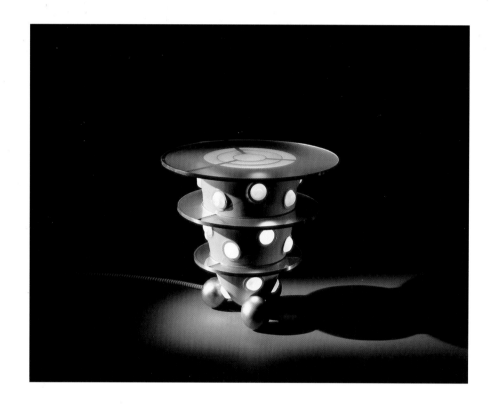

Kinoko, 1992
Stehleuchte, floor lamp, lampadaire

Design Hironen

p. 175
Dentist's Lamp, 1992
Stehleuchte, floor lamp, lampadaire

Design Hironen

FOTONACHWEIS

CREDITS

CRÉDITS PHOTOGRAPHIQUES

Satashi Asakawa	2
Hiroyuki Hirai	30 o., 40, 41, 69, 70, 71, 72, 170, 172
Masayuki Hayashi	30 u., 31
Nacasa	34, 36, 37, 38, 39, 42, 43, 58, 59, 102, 103, 104, 105, 108, 109, 174, 175
Yoshiho Shiratori	49, 50, 51, 52, 53, 56, 57, 60, 61
Mitsumasa Fujitsuka	66, 67, 68, 70 o., 80, 81, 118, 119
Bin Asakawa	73, 74, 77, 78 & 79, 143, 145, 160, 161
Keiicki Tahara	75
Shigeru Ohno	88, 89, 90, 91, 92, 93, 94, 95
Hiroshi Ueda	96, 97
Takayuki Ogawa	106, 110, 111
Tahara Keiichi	142
Yoshio Takase	144
Kenichi Suzuki	152 & 153
Fujitsuka Mitsumasa	168, 169
Makoto Sei Watanabe	171
Iwama Akinori	173

Der Verlag dankt allen Designern, Architekten und Firmen für ihre freundliche Unterstützung. Insbesondere möchten wir uns bei Frau Masae Ueki und Herrn Yasuo Satomi bedanken.

The publishers wishes to thank all of the designers, architects and firms for their gracious assistance. We are especially indebted to Ms. Masae Ueki and Mr. Yasuo Satomi.

Les Éditions remercient tous les designers, architectes et entreprises et tout particulièrement Madame Masae Ueki et Monsieur Yasuo Satomi pour leur soutien amical.